Emotional
Wisdom®

Emotional Wisdom®

A Compassionate Guide to the Messages Hidden in Your Feelings

Harriet Haberman, Ph.D.

ITH Publications
Fort Lee, New Jersey

The stories and vignettes in this book are composite and fictionalized sketches to protect the anonymity of any particular individual. The ideas in this book are based on the author's clinical experience with individuals, couples, and empowerment groups. Therefore, they are not intended as a substitute for psychotherapy or other professional services. The reader should consult a qualified mental health care professional or other competent professionals in the event that any particular symptoms may require diagnosis, therapy, or medical attention.

Although the author and publisher have made every effort to ensure the accuracy and completeness of information contained in this book, we assume no responsibility for errors, inaccuracies, omissions, or any inconsistency herein. Any slighting of people, places, or organizations is unintentional.

Emotional Wisdom® is the trademarked property of
Harriet Haberman, Ph.D., and ITH Publications.

Front cover photo by David Sultanik
Author's photo by Roberto Rabanne

Second printing 2008
ISBN 978-0-9762223-7-8
LCCN 2007940411

DEDICATION

This book is dedicated to my clients for opening their hearts, allowing me the privilege of sharing their inner journey, and trusting my ability to guide them toward personal growth and empowerment.

Harriet Haberman, Ph.D.

CONTENTS

MAKING THE CHANGES LAST

FOREWORD

H arriet Haberman's book, *Emotional Wisdom: A Compassionate Guide to the Messages Hidden in Your Feelings*, is rich with the wisdom of a loving and seasoned therapist. This insightful book fills in the vital gap left by so many authors and experts that *only* emphasize and focus on the power of our positive thoughts and feelings—reinforcing the age-old temptation to believe that by willing ourselves to think and feel positively we can overcome all obstacles in our path. Dr. Haberman helps us to recognize the difference between thoughts and feelings and to acknowledge the undeniable truth of the greater potency and power of our emotions. More importantly, she encourages and inspires us to participate in the process that is so often overlooked—the willingness to tap into even those feelings that we perceive as negative, so that we might learn how to reclaim the energy tied to our denied emotions. She reminds us again and again of our right to heal from the lost messages of love (denied love, lost love, abused love, and the list goes on) in order to find the release we need for the journey of full transformation.

As a long-time traveler on the road of self-awareness, I found myself irresistibly drawn to look again into the realm of my feelings, particularly those emotions that my defenses still help me to dismiss and avoid. The warmth of her writing and the confidence of her skill inspire an immediate impulse to apply her techniques and tools. Dr. Haberman communicates throughout her book that by compassionately learning what all our feelings are trying to say, we fill in the missing part of the equation necessary to manifest the goals we seek. She then guides us to engage this rewarding process, allowing us to reclaim the empowerment we need to actualize our dreams and find lasting fulfillment.

I believe you will discover in her writing the qualities that most of us are looking for when we seek out a therapist: a compassionate person who patiently helps us open to the mystery of our own lives with a sense of understanding, self-acceptance, and confidence that real change is possible. Initially, as you embark on the journey of greater self-discovery, you will find that she offers a comprehensive map describing the nature and influence emotions play in our lives. Her illuminating vignettes of case studies demonstrate with remarkable clarity how the untapped resources of our emotions can either keep us trapped in self-destructive patterns or be used to steer our lives toward our goals and happiness. She brilliantly weaves insights, case examples, and exercises to inspire the reader, no matter how experienced, to want to look more deeply into this wonderful well of wisdom we all have.

Finally, Dr. Haberman offers a series of accessible and time-tested tools to circumvent the conscious mind and make direct contact with the messages our feelings are trying to communicate. On each step of the journey you will notice the clarity and support that can only come from a compassionate and competent therapist. Her writing style reflects her warmth, interest, encouragement, and skill, and we are all the richer for her wise and generous counsel.

Eleanor Payson, L.M.S.W., A.C.S.W.
Royal Oak, Michigan

ACKNOWLEDGMENTS

When I first decided to write this book, I had some notion of what the process entailed. I had already published a booklet, as well as numerous articles. However, a book, by its nature, is grander in scope, and consequently, so are the number of people necessary for its successful completion. It is for this reason that I wish to acknowledge all those whose contributions and support have been a crucial part of my journey. No matter how large or small, each unique piece was carefully woven into the book's fabric and valuable to its accomplishment.

Although I have always been a perpetual student, it was only after an epiphany in 1991 that the course of my life, as well as my work, took a dramatic turn. Simply put, I realized that my choices had been influenced primarily by the approval of others and that such decisions needed to be refocused, based on my own needs. This concept, which seems so obvious, was no longer just a logical understanding; it resonated in every fiber of my being. Based on my epiphany, I was drawn to experiences that enhanced this awareness, and consequently, some of the professional training that followed had far-reaching effects. As well as significantly shaping my personal growth, these experiences and professional opportunities contributed to my educational development, eventual refinement of the Emotional Wisdom process, and writing of this book. Equally important were the insights and understandings that powerfully threaded themselves into my essence. I began with wonderful workshops at Kripalu Center for Yoga and Health, in Lenox, Massachusetts. I attended numerous seminars during the early to mid 1990s, which covered a wide range of experiential trainings. All were presented by extraordinarily skilled and compassionate instructors.

Concurrent with my work at Kripalu, I studied cognitive behavioral therapy with Jeffery Young, Ph.D. His work, Schema Focused Therapy, introduced me to another approach in healing. In addition, his seminar indirectly led me to my next influential teacher, Harville Hendrix, Ph.D., founder of Imago Therapy. His brilliant methodology, complemented by experiential skill-building techniques, remains an integral part of my clinical practice. I was also fortunate to have been personally trained by him.

Following my experiences at Kripalu, I explored the wonderful work of Drs. Gay and Kathlyn Hendricks. Through their profound and inspiring theories, I deepened my knowledge and interpretation of the body-mind connection. As part of one of their trainings, I participated in rebirthing, which proved to be truly transformative.

After integrating the knowledge I had experientially acquired, I took two levels of training in Eye Movement Desensitization and Reprocessing, commonly referred to as EMDR. This amazing work was founded by Francine Shapiro, Ph.D. The power of release and healing through this approach is often remarkable. I continue to use EMDR as a primary staple in my experiential toolbox.

Bringing these skills to clients has been so extraordinarily rewarding that I wanted to share my accumulated knowledge and experience with others. Therefore, I realized I would have to put my thoughts on paper. Translating one's ideas and actually creating a book indeed involve a journey. This would not have been possible without the logistical help of some creative people. For editorial assistance, I would like to thank Lori Murray for editing the first draft of the book. Also, I owe special thanks and appreciation to Maureen Buchanan Jones, Ph.D., for her editorial ability in gently and wisely guiding me to complete the finished product. For helping me eliminate the final kinks, I wish to express gratitude to Barry Scheinkopf and Cathy Bowman. A special acknowledgment is also due to Sharon Sharp, Ph.D., for adding the finishing editorial polish to the manuscript. In addition, I want to thank Cathy Bowman for designing the layout and cover; her contribution is always valued. I would also like to acknowledge Carolyn Francavilla, my office assistant, for capably wearing many hats throughout this project. Also, I want to thank David Sultanik for the generous offer of his beautiful front-cover photograph and for his other helpful contributions to ensure this project's successful completion. An additional acknowledgment is due to Michael Green, who graciously helped me design a pathway for the book's birth into the world.

A special thank you is due to my dear friend Maryann Ciraulo for reading the first, as well as the final copy of the book, and for continuously believing in me. Furthermore, I wish to acknowledge good friends Eleanor Kessler and Carol Porter for reading the galley proofs and offering their helpful suggestions. Deep gratitude goes to my devoted friend Eleanor Payson. Her faith in me, along with her support and wise counsel, has been an invaluable guiding light throughout the process. She generously shared her own journey as a writer, to help pave the way for mine.

However, most of all, I want to thank those whose presence has deeply touched my being: specifically, my beloved parents; my dearly loved daughter, Rebecca; my family of friends; and the spiritual guidance I have been blessed to receive. Their love remains, as always, the cornerstone in my life.

LIST OF CLIENT EXAMPLES

LIST OF EXPERIENTIAL EXERCISES

PREFACE

A good friend of mine, a creative, successful businessman in his mid forties, made what he considered a poor choice in a recent relationship. He met someone, became totally infatuated, and within three weeks had asked this person to move in with him. About a month later, he was having serious second thoughts. His comment was, "I don't understand how someone as intelligent as I am could do something so stupid!"

The statement was all too familiar. Over the years I have heard variations of this theme from clients, friends, and family alike. The truth is that such decisions do not stem from stupidity but rather from not understanding the hidden meaning of our emotions and, consequently, ourselves. *Most of us have not been taught techniques to access this important information.* However, once we realize that emotions are *always* attempting to teach and wisely guide us, there is a greater likelihood that we will be receptive to the process. The good news is that at any point, each of us *can* acquire skills to decipher the valuable messages our feelings offer.

The purpose of this book is to help you do precisely that. It provides specific methods that allow you to begin or enrich the process of emotional healing. Examples of these techniques include learning how to interpret the meaning of your emotions, developing compassion for whatever arises, and creating action

1

steps to transform your life. Also incorporated are experiential exercises and client examples, as well as final tips to support your process. Since these skills can get to the heart of an issue quickly, the process is ideal for short-term work. The client examples throughout the book will effectively illustrate how rapidly the process can succeed, as well as the value of accessing your emotional wisdom. The result of implementing these procedures will be greater balance, contentment, and inner peace.

The skills involved in the Emotional Wisdom process are worthwhile for everyone. There is no doubt that you need to understand your emotions. As psychologist Nathaniel Brandon, in his book *The Power of Self-Esteem*, states:

> Most of us are children of dysfunctional families. I do not mean that most of us had alcoholic parents or were sexually or otherwise abused or that we grew up in an atmosphere of physical violence. I mean that most of us grew up in homes characterized by conflicting signals, denials of reality, parental lying, and a lack of adequate respect for our mind and person. I am speaking of the *average* person.

If you are thinking of exploring personal growth, *Emotional Wisdom: A Compassionate Guide to the Messages Hidden in Your Feelings* can be an introduction to understanding the significant benefit of dealing with your feelings. If you are already on the path, it can provide helpful tools to enrich your journey.

Recently, worldwide interest has emerged regarding what has been called the law of attraction. The concept was popularized in *The Secret*, by Rhonda Byrne. In essence, the law states that what we think, consciously or unconsciously, we will attract. However, there is also a powerful association between what we think and what we feel. As Byrne states, "Emotions are valuable tools that instantly tell us what we are thinking." Michael

Bernard Beckwith, founder of Agape International Spiritual Center and contributor to *The Secret*, adds, "This is a feeling Universe. If you just intellectually believe something, but you have no corresponding feeling underneath that, you don't necessarily have enough power to manifest what you want in your life." Jack Canfield, author, motivational speaker, and another contributor states, "It is the feeling that really creates the attraction, not just the picture or the thought."

This is where the Emotional Wisdom process can serve as a useful adjunct to the concept of the law of attraction. The goals of both are complementary: to cleanse the feeling and thinking traps that prevent individuals from shaping their lives in a positive direction. This book will allow you to accomplish this by offering *practical, simple applications* for the awareness and interpretation of your emotional messages. Sadly, these messages are all too often neglected or ignored, keeping you trapped in a destructive cycle. In turn, this process blocks a clear pathway to the law of attraction. Only when the messages are correctly interpreted and reframed can the core energy be transformed. This book offers you a process that reveals the positive desire underlying the negativity, so as to create momentum toward transformation. As you will see in chapter 8, the Emotional Wisdom process allows you to clarify and align your feelings with your thoughts and actions. This approach, in turn, provides the power to attract what you want in any situation. In addition, Emotional Wisdom compassionately encourages the development of self-acceptance throughout the process.

One final note: This book contains exercises at the end of each chapter that are meant to deepen your understanding of the material discussed in the text. If you are ready to experience shifts in your perception and feeling, it is highly recommended that you do the exercises. Only then can permanent transformation begin, because *healing must occur on both the verbal and nonverbal levels.* As you will learn in chapter 3, the root of most

3

emotional wounding is housed in the portion of the brain that has no speech. Therefore, without healing on a nonverbal level, theories may be interesting and even somewhat helpful, but lasting change is unlikely.

When you do the exercises, remember that creating a feeling of safety is a significant part of the Emotional Wisdom process. However, if doing these exercises on your own does not seem comfortable, especially if you are new to personal growth, do not feel obligated to complete them. Instead, just notice what emotions come up for you as you read the exercises and honor whatever your feelings are. Also, be aware that some of the activities described in the book, such as the exercises cited in client examples, generally require the assistance of a skilled professional. Others, such as those outlined in the three-step healing process and the seven skills for resolving present problems, can be done on your own or with a close friend. However, if overwhelming emotions arise, it is highly recommended that you seek professional guidance.

After the last chapter, you will find a group of blank pages, titled "Reflections," where you can make notes as you read this book. You may find it helpful to record whatever associations emerge as you read, as well as to explore more extensively your thoughts and feelings arising from the end-of-chapter exercises. If you choose to reread the book or redo the exercises, your writings on the "Reflections" pages will provide a valuable record of your initial responses to the material. Taking the time to explore your responses in writing can help you compassionately appreciate your individual journey toward healing and wholeness.

Above all, remember to be gentle with yourself. Honor who you are now, as well as your potential self. The concepts in this book are here to support and guide you, wherever you are in your journey. My hope is that what you learn will enhance a voyage of empowerment and compassion for the most important person in your life—YOU!

An Overview of Emotional Wisdom

CHAPTER 1

A Process That Helps You Heal

The concept of Emotional Wisdom evolved from my thirty-plus years of working with many hundreds of clients and observing which techniques helped them positively transform their lives. What emerged was a healing model that includes a series of simple yet powerful tools and a variety of experiential exercises. The results provide a sense of true empowerment and improved self-esteem. In addition, the Emotional Wisdom process offers three new concepts:

- *Emotions have their own logic.* The popular myth is that feelings are illogical and that emotional intensity is related to some type of personal instability. In truth, feelings are logical, and you need only learn the skills to unlock their healing power. More about this concept appears in chapter 3.

- *Emotions are neither good nor bad.* The prevailing myth is that some feelings—anger, fear, and sadness, for example—are not welcome or are to be quickly eliminated. In truth, these emotions are simply primitive messengers trying to provide you, as best they can, with helpful advice, no matter how unpleasant the emotions may initially feel. These issues are further discussed in chapter 4.

- *Honoring and accepting old behavioral patterns are crucial to lasting change.* The popular myth is that once you are aware of negative behaviors, you must "get rid of them." Not only is this impossible, but such an attempt can evoke anger, shame, and guilt, in turn undermining the possibility of enduring transformation. More about this concept appears in chapter 7.

The Emotional Wisdom approach described in this book also teaches you to more effectively manage future problems by discovering how to sidestep familiar behavioral traps and create healthier new responses. The possibility of understanding your emotions is available to you at any age. It is merely your choice to learn the skills that decipher their valuable messages!

The Principles of Emotional Wisdom

Three introductory principles best describe Emotional Wisdom. After outlining all of them, a client example is presented to demonstrate each of the tenets.

1. Emotional Wisdom is a healing model based on learning.

Historically, psychological treatment was founded on the medical model, which is based on eliminating symptoms. According to this view, the heart of healing is the doctor-patient relationship, where the doctor is regarded as the authority. The client, better known in this paradigm as "the patient," is viewed by the doctor and society as being psychologically deficient or nonfunctioning. The primary focus is on logical thought and deductive reasoning; therefore, clients only *talk* about their problems. A cure is thought to be achieved by understanding the issue and its associations from their past. This method is commonly known as "talk therapy."

In sharp contrast, the Emotional Wisdom process offers a healing model based on learning. It offers skills that teach you to effectively understand and *manage* your feelings, as opposed to unrealistically trying to eliminate them. From this paradigm, the relationship between the individual seeking to heal, known as "the client," and the therapist is collaborative and participatory. The client's issues are not viewed as signs of dysfunction but as *opportunities* to learn and grow. Therefore, the therapist doesn't "cure" the client but instead facilitates healing by helping the client access inner feelings and transform that knowledge into practical action steps. This healing is accomplished by experiential exercises as well as talking. The experiential work includes a range of possibilities, such as guided imagery (including inner child work), Eye Movement Desensitization and Reprocessing (EMDR), breath work, body-mind awareness, and hypnosis. These experiences gently bypass the conscious mind and open pathways to your inner emotional world, which contains your deepest truths. Once this information emerges, you can apply the messages and reframe your thinking. The case example at the end of the chapter illustrates this progression.

2. Emotional Wisdom includes a simple three-step process to heal old wounds.

The first step in the threefold process is awareness; this includes understanding the problem, its origins, and its ways of having artfully woven itself into your life. The second step is loving self-acceptance, which is essential no matter what has occurred. Making peace with yourself is often the most difficult component because of the profound self-criticism and self-loathing that exist in us all. *Self-compassion is the crucial element needed for change to occur.* The third step is to create and implement specific action plans. This is also necessary to concretely manifest the transformation you desire. It is important to note that no matter who is using the Emotional Wisdom process, the approach remains the same, although the steps may vary according to the need of each individual. More about the threefold process is provided in chapter 7.

As stated, Emotional Wisdom helps you heal old wounds. However, most of us resist exploring them, because of their likely connection to our childhood. We desperately want to believe that whatever occurred long ago is over and of no consequence in the present. In addition, we are apt to be distracted by current life events such as completing an education, building a career, finding a life partner, starting a family, or moving into a new community. Although these are noble pursuits, they can and often do create a veil of protection from internal issues that yearn to be acknowledged.

Reflection evolves—most often uninvited—through a life crisis. This crisis generally takes place anywhere between the late thirties to early fifties and is often related to some type of change or loss. The crisis could be triggered by a job (being demoted, changing careers, or even getting a new or better job), a relationship (losing one, finding one, or having a significant shift in an existing one), health (problems with your own health and/or that of those close to you), or an encounter with the death of someone dear. The profound shock can affect you in two ways. The first is a deep sense of loss that is specifically related to the crisis and lessens over time with little or no major change in your existence. The second spirals you into a vortex of reflective examination of your life. In this latter occurrence, what emerges is often startling. Generally, the surprising revelation is that there have been a host of similar behavioral patterns in times of crisis and loss. These have artfully threaded themselves throughout your past; the only difference lies in the particular scenarios and faces you have encountered.

3. Emotional Wisdom teaches you to decipher the messages hidden in your feelings.

In the following chapters you will see how you have become a master at skillfully creating a web of words that keep your feelings at bay. You are often unaware that *your emotions, not your words,* reflect your highest truths. Instead, you find yourself unconsciously compelled by potent yet seemingly unknown forces—in reality, your feelings—that ensnare you in a "victim position." This sense of helplessness, which is both familiar and frustrating, traps you in a powerful vise, often for a lifetime. The antidotes to this helplessness are the healing aspects of Emotional Wisdom. Essential is the development of safety, which is described in detail in the third section of the book. Also introduced in this section are Emotional Wisdom's seven simple skills. Incorporating them will help you quickly heal *any* situation or problem manifesting in your present life. These techniques encompass all that has been taught in the previous chapters. Combined with the threefold process of awareness, acceptance, and action, they form the heart of Emotional Wisdom. The easy, practical skills quickly bring you to the core of the issue, and they help you formulate an action step to move you in your desired direction. The client examples woven throughout will illustrate that although you may be initially disconnected from your deepest truths, there are specific techniques to reconnect yourself and heal.

Exploring the Emotional Wisdom Process: Susan

Susan, a kindly grandmother in her late fifties, sought to do some personal work on lifelong feelings of rejection and low self-esteem. Since her children were no longer living at home, Susan felt she had the opportunity to do something for herself. She began reflecting on her long-term negative beliefs and decided it was time to change. Her hope was to understand the uncomfortable emotions that plagued her, as well as formulate an action plan to transform them.

This was the first time that Susan had done any psychological exploration, and initially she did not want to reveal much about herself. However, after a session or two, she became more comfortable talking about her life. This comfort was evident from what she said, as well as from her body language. Susan soon came into the office with shoulders more relaxed, less bodily fidgeting, and a softening of her facial expressions. Slowly, she began to open up about her past.

Susan was severely asthmatic as a child. She grew up feeling defective and unable to please others. These emotions did not make sense to her, since she portrayed her background as "normal" and her parents as involved and caring. However, she did state that her mother was not particularly warm or demonstrative and, at times, could be critical. Susan had a nagging sense of being unloved by her mother, although she had no concrete evidence to support her claim. Despite her sense of low self-esteem, she had achieved a level of academic and professional success. She was a respected university professor for many years. In addition, Susan had what she described as "a fairly good marriage of almost forty years" and three grown daughters. Yet she felt intimidated in many of her relationships within and outside the family. Susan said that she was still always trying to please, often at her own expense.

With her comfort level established, I discussed the possibility of doing an experiential exercise. The purpose of this work was to see if we could more efficiently access the origins of Susan's belief system. She agreed, and I chose guided imagery, in which the client remains fully awake and aware throughout the process. The purpose of guided imagery, as with all experiential exercises, is to bypass the conscious mind and tap into our emotions. This direct access to feelings is critical for healing, since the conscious mind is ruled by the intellect, whereas our early wounds are governed by powerful, unconscious feelings. The results of the imagery frequently offer stunning associations, which previously were unlinked in the conscious mind.

I led Susan through steps I typically use during the guided imagery process. While she was seated, I asked her to keep her eyes closed, to minimize external distractions. Before initiating guided imagery, I asked Susan to select an issue. I then introduced the Healing Breath, a breathing exercise that is outlined at the end of this chapter. Once I sensed that she was relaxed, I read a script that I had specifically created for the situation. Through the vehicle of imagery, Susan was then gently guided so that communication could occur with her inner wisdom.

Susan chose to explore why she perceived herself as being unlovable to her mother. She was successful in visualizing a safe place that included a screen on which to view the scenes of the imagery script. On the screen, she visualized herself as a three-year-old in her childhood bedroom. In the scene, she was having a severe asthmatic attack and reported that she was terrified as she struggled to breathe. Her mother was in the room and was attempting various medical interventions to relieve Susan's anguish. In the imagery, her mother wore the same expression Susan had seen many times in childhood. There were deep creases in her mother's forehead, her eyes were open wide and gazing intently at Susan, and her mouth was tightly clenched. Previously, Susan had interpreted this look as one of annoyance or rejection. In the scene, as her mother anxiously tried to help, Susan suddenly had a shocking realization. What she had previously interpreted as her mother's rejection now had a new connotation. For the first time, Susan was able to understand that her mother's face reflected worry. It was the look of a parent with a sickly child and was not related to Susan's lovability. Her comment was, "Although she wasn't very warm, I can sense from the

picture on the screen that my mother did love me!" That awareness, although pleasing to her, was also troubling. All her life, she
had associated her mother's expressions with the incorrect assumption that she was defective and unlovable.

As an adult, Susan transferred this powerful supposition to
her other relationships and created lifelong unhappiness. It took
numerous sessions for her to integrate this new awareness. She
also worked to develop compassion for her earlier perception
and its enduring consequences. In addition, we created small,
specific action steps to empower Susan. She was able to begin
creating boundaries with others and learn more about her own
needs. Over time, she observed the positive effects these steps
had on her relationships.

As Susan's example illustrates, the Emotional Wisdom process, offers resources that allow you to safely revisit the area of
wounding, fortified with tools, skills, and support that allow
emotional release and healing to occur. In the next chapter I
explore and explain precisely why emotions have this command-
ing influence.

The Healing Breath

Facilitating transformation means bypassing the distractions
of the conscious mind and allowing you to access and decipher
the wisdom within. To assist this process, I've added experiential exercises at the end of each chapter. It will be helpful for
you to read the exercises a few times before you try to do them.

This first exercise is an excellent way to quickly center yourself and increase your ability to concentrate and focus. It clears
mental clutter and allows you greater clarity for realizing the
right path for you in any situation. It can be done anywhere;
simply find a place where you will not be disturbed. This exer-

cise is not to be used when visual impairment is unsafe for you or others, such as while driving or operating machinery. The exercise can be completed within one to three minutes, depending on how much time you wish to allow. Initially, you will have to use a watch or timer to estimate the time. After you've become more familiar with the exercise, this will no longer be necessary. Now let us begin.

Decide now if you wish to use this technique for sharpening your focus or clarifying an issue. Remember, you can vary the purpose each time you do it. Close your eyes and make yourself comfortable. Gently squeeze your entire body, tightening your face, shoulders, arms, legs, hands, and torso. As you take your next breath, let go of your muscle tension and feel yourself release as much stress as you comfortably can. Take another breath and release even more. Now pick a color that is particularly soothing. If no color comes to mind, that's okay; simply focus on a golden light. If a color does come to mind, select a shade of the color that feels particularly nourishing. Surround yourself with this color. Inhale and mentally say the word *in*. As you exhale, mentally say the word *out*. Stay with the process of the breath for one to three minutes, allowing both the color and the words to soothe, nurture, and protect you. Gently open your eyes.

If you are using this exercise for overall clarity, it may feel as if someone has cleansed your mental lens. If you are using it regarding a specific issue, go back to the original subject. Often a response different from what you'd anticipated may seem to "pop into your head." That response may be coming from your inner knowing, so give it some consideration!

The Power
of Emotions

CHAPTER 2

The Profound Effect of Feelings on Everyday Life

A fter more than thirty years of practice, I remain in awe of the power of emotions and their influence on our lives. Repeatedly, clients report the damaging effects that result from being out of touch with their emotional messages. That is why Emotional Wisdom is so crucial: it is the antidote to our historical beliefs about emotions.

The prevailing principle has been that feelings are to be ignored rather than understood. Early in our lives, parents, caregivers, and society teach us how *not* to deal with our emotions. We constantly are given messages such as "It's not nice to get angry" or "You shouldn't feel that way" or "If you don't stop crying, I'll give you something to cry about!" Displays of so-called negative feelings such as anger, fear, and sadness are generally intolerable to our caregivers, and even intense joy can be unacceptable. This reaction stems from the caregivers' lack of skills in handling *their own* emotions. When they see a youngster having a powerful display of feelings, the occurrence becomes a threatening, often unconscious reflection of their own repression and denial. In order to deal with their anxiety, caretakers insist that the child get rid of her* feelings as quickly as possible,

---

*For the sake of clarity and ease, the pronoun *she* will be used throughout this chapter to designate both genders.

which often means the child receives some type of reprimand. In turn, the message given to the child is that feelings are bad. Since feelings are an integral part of her being, the youngster internalizes the belief to mean *I am bad.*

Paradoxically, it is precisely those hidden emotions that represent her deepest truth and authentic self. The youngster surrenders her authenticity in response to the most primitive and powerful human instinct, survival. We know that food, water, and shelter are essential to stay alive, but we may not realize that love and approval are just as vital. The Harlow monkey experiments clearly illustrated this principle.

Dr. Harry Harlow was an American psychologist whose famous monkey studies, using a wire monkey "mother" versus the real monkey mother, demonstrated that the need for affectionate interaction with the real mother was as critical to healthy development as was the physical need for food. In the studies, some baby monkeys were separated from their mothers within a few hours of birth and placed with wire replicas. These wire monkey "mothers" had a bottle placed within the wire to provide the infant monkeys with nourishment. However, with no touch, interaction, or affection, the baby monkeys suffered severely delayed development. Harlow also noted what he referred to as "strange atypical behavioral patterns" that resulted in isolation and aggressive actions. Many of these monkeys became socially inept and were often unsuccessful at mating. Those who did have offspring were often negligent or abusive to their young, resulting in the baby monkeys' death.

Although a child instinctively knows that her continued existence depends on adult approval, she is oblivious of the price. The cost is self-alienation that evolves into a threefold path of pain, blame, and shame. The following discussion elaborates how this develops. Pain—specifically, psychic pain—occurs because the youngster does not perceive that it is safe to feel or express her emotions. Therefore, the child is forced to bury or numb them.

Blame involves the child's development of self-blame for even having what she believes are unsafe feelings and the desire to express them. The child's general thought is that she *shouldn't* feel what she is feeling or, at the very least, that she should be able to handle her feelings by herself. If she can't, the youngster believes it is her fault, and any expression of these feelings will result in being rejected by the significant others in her world.

Shame is the outcome of both pain and blame. The child perceives that having "unsafe feelings" and needing to express them are wrong or shameful. Unconsciously, the child believes that she must be flawed because what she feels is incorrect. Underlying all three components is a sense of defectiveness. Thus, the path of pain, blame, and shame emerges.

The high level of anguish that results from this threefold process is generally handled by seeking out another behavior whose purpose is to soothe and numb the pain. For example, if the child chooses food as a source of self-soothing, food takes on an association as a resource to alleviate pain. Food is then sought when any type of uncomfortable situation arises. Although appeasing, it is only a short-term solution until the next episode of self-alienation begins. Eventually, whatever refuge the child has chosen takes on a life of its own, generally with powerful negative consequences. It is precisely this progression that is the root of all addictions such as those involving drugs, alcohol, gambling and sex.

In addition, these addictive patterns are reinforced as the child imitates the coping strategies exhibited by the wounded, oblivious adults in her world. A child's teachers are everywhere. They model how *not* to cope with emotions, and they remain in constant states of being victimized, helpless, angry, and depressed.

For relief, the child notices them turning to a variety of outlets, including food, alcohol, gambling, negative beliefs, or bad relationships. Remember, the purpose of these behaviors initially does not stem from a desire to be self-destructive but rather from a yearning to seek relief from unbearable feelings. Since the youngster rarely has an opportunity to discover alternatives, these constant states of learned distractions quickly become second nature to her. Without realizing it, the child is reinforced in seeking out addictive outlets.

Before proceeding, there is an important point worth noting. It is virtually impossible for *any* caregiver to be 100 percent present to a child's needs 100 percent of the time. Even in the most loving of homes, where parents are very focused on their child, many other distractions are present. Examples of these include the needs of other family members such as one's spouse, siblings, and aging parents; financial pressures; health concerns; and social climate, which would include war and other catastrophes. Having *every one* of our basic requirements—food, water, shelter, and warmth— unconditionally met happens only in the womb. There, our needs are always taken care of, and the only requirement is just to be. After birth we unconsciously yearn to replicate this glorious state and often spend the rest of our lives desperately trying to recapture it. When this does not happen, we get angry or sad and feel unloved. Thus, in a nutshell, none of us escapes some degree of psychological injury. It is inevitable.

Using Addiction to Suppress Emotional Pain: Rhonda

Rhonda, an attractive, personable woman in her forties, grew up in a home with an alcoholic father. He was excessively critical of her, and he consistently conveyed that she wasn't good enough. Any of her attempts to prove otherwise were met by his intense anger and severe tantrums. Over time, Rhonda became addicted to this negative belief system.

She believed her father's criticisms because, like all young children, she viewed her parents as omnipotent and infallible. Parents are *supposed* to have their child's best interest at heart, so how could her father's reactions be anything but accurate? It would be devastating to Rhonda, or any youngster, to believe that a parent's comments were intentionally unloving. This realization would be experienced as a devastating betrayal of a parent's role. Thus, Rhonda felt overwhelmingly sad, helpless, and trapped. Also, the betrayal can be unconsciously experienced as a threat to our assumption of how the family system is *supposed to be*. In Rhonda's case, she unconsciously felt more secure if she believed she was defective, rather than acknowledging that the problem was her father's. This belief allowed for the possibility of hope and change. Rhonda's perception was that if she could modify *her* behavior, her dad would see her in a more affirmative light. Once this modification occurred, she felt his responses to her would be positively transformed.

As a child, Rhonda spent a great deal of time trying to make herself acceptable, lovable, and "good enough" in her dad's eyes. However, no matter what she did, she was unsuccessful. Rhonda's coping mechanism for her deep disappointment became withdrawal and a sense of hopelessness. She eventually internalized that his damaging allegations were true. As a result of the childhood encounters with her father, Rhonda became addicted to a negative belief system. She perceived that in any difficult interaction, she was defective and at fault.

Rhonda did not realize that the consequences of these early dynamics were profoundly evident in adulthood. She unconsciously developed a lifelong defense of not responding to controversy and assumed that any negative feedback was accurate. As a result, she withdrew from people. Rhonda's liaisons with men became a glaring mirror of her relationship to her father. The men she became involved with tended to be emotionally abusive and echoed the sentiments her father had ingrained. Therefore, if any problems in the relationship emerged, Rhonda held herself responsible.

This assumption was the presenting issue when she came to my office. Rhonda was having serious difficulties with her significant other and sought counseling to "fix" her problems. Rhonda believed her relationship would be healed once she learned the necessary skills. In time, she was able to recognize that her negative belief system was the real issue. She initially struggled to accept the deeper truth: her father's intense criticisms originated from his own profound early wounding and not from any defect in her character. His self-hatred, deep sadness, and overwhelming fear were the source of his alcoholism and intense dissatisfaction with his own life. They were also the basis of his critical behavior toward his daughter.

Rhonda also became aware that her childhood feeling of being defective was identical to her father's early experiences. Alcoholism and disparaging conduct toward children were common threads on her father's side of the family. Her paternal grandmother had shown unrelenting disapproval of Rhonda's father throughout his life. Since her grandmother lived well into her nineties, Rhonda was able to observe her father's and grandmother's interactions. She witnessed her grandmother daily reprimanding and chastising her father. In addition, she recalled hearing that this same pattern of adult verbal abuse and alcoholic behavior had occurred in at least two previous generations.

As a result of our work, Rhonda became aware of the profound effect of familial behavioral patterns. Some experiential work to bypass the conscious mind helped her release old messages of inadequacy. From this, Rhonda was able to change the way she perceived these early messages. In addition, we formulated small action steps to change her behavior. Instead of isolating herself, she began to reach out to others for support and comfort. When necessary, she also began to assert herself. The new experiences gave Rhonda confidence. These perceptions and behavioral changes helped her slowly detach from her childhood belief system. She was able to transform her feelings of defectiveness to empowerment. Realizing that her boyfriend was unwilling to let go of his blaming behavior, Rhonda ended the relationship. This choice further enhanced her sense of self-esteem.

Rhonda's case also demonstrates that family patterns profoundly influence behavior. The blueprints get handed down from generation to generation like an unwanted heirloom. In order to break this cycle, we need to learn skills that will allow us to recognize and reframe these emotional messages. If we do not, we will continue on the path of unconscious distractions and addictions.

There is a high price to pay for such self-destructive behaviors. The cost affects almost every aspect of our lives, including our physical health. In his groundbreaking book *Emotional Intelligence*, psychologist and lecturer Daniel Goleman demonstrated that it is our emotions, not our thoughts, that rule our lives. Our feelings pervade every aspect of our being, including our health. Goleman stated: "Helping people better manage their upsetting feelings—anger, anxiety, depression, pessimism and loneliness—is a form of disease prevention." The World Health Organization reports that the second leading cause of death in the year 2020, after heart disease, will no longer be cancer but depression-based illness.

Goleman cited another significant study done by psychologist Robert Adler, which showed that the immune system is capable of learning. The research revealed that the immune system *can* learn to change responses to emotional stimuli because the immune system and central nervous system interact. The movie *What the Bleep Do We Know!?* also touches on the brain's ability to form new emotional pathways. This is hopeful and exciting news. It implies that improved techniques for dealing with feelings can positively influence our physical health. Understanding the body-mind connection is essential.

Feelings manifest themselves through body language and are a highly accurate reflection of your emotional state. It takes just a brief example to demonstrate this profound truth. Suppose you walk into a room and see someone you know. She is perspiring, her face is turning red, veins in her neck are protruding, and she is clenching her fists. You ask the individual if she is angry. If she replies, "Yes," then her words and body language are in sync and reinforce the reality of what you have witnessed. However, if the person replies, "No!" what do you believe? There is an apparent discrepancy in what you are witnessing and what you are being told. Do you trust the words or the body language? The answer has its roots in our childhood quest for survival. In that vulnerable situation, we quickly learn to trust whatever cues are necessary to ensure our continued existence. We soon discover that what is manifested through body language gives us more accurate information than the spoken word. The body *always* reflects our deepest emotions, even when we are consciously unaware of them.

Emotions are generally associated with specific bodily reactions. The following simple correlations, which are adapted from Gay and Kathlyn Hendricks's work on the existing general body responses to feelings that may help you expand your self-knowledge.

- *Sadness*—Pay particular attention to the front of your body, down the midline from throat to belly. This is a zone where many people experience their sadness.

- *Anger*—Pay attention to the neck and shoulders, as these are areas where many people experience their anger.

- *Fear*—Pay particular attention to jitters or butterflies in the stomach, sweaty palms, or a nauseous feeling. These are sensory indicators of fear.

- *Joy*—Pay particular attention to overall muscle relaxation and sense of peace. This is how most people bodily express their joy.

You have seen the possibility of learning to understand your body-mind associations and their related emotions. It has also been evident that applying these skills can bring relief from longstanding wounds. If this is so, the question remains, why are more people not choosing this path? The next chapter sheds light on this.

Identifying Feelings in Your Body: A Tool for Healing

To decipher the wisdom that emotions offer, it's important to identify how a feeling expresses itself in your body. This identification can be healing because body sensations are true indicators of emotions and have important messages. The following exercise will help you deepen your awareness of these significant associations.

Review the Healing Breath exercise outlined at the end of chapter 1. Now sit comfortably, close your eyes, and repeat the steps. After you have done the process for one to three minutes, select a feeling from the following four: anger, fear, sadness, or joy. Each feeling has a specific way it affects you; certain muscles tense when you are angry, while others tense when you are afraid or sad. The more you learn about each of these feelings, the better you will be able to identify and deal with them in real-life situations.

After you have chosen a feeling, keep your eyes closed and think of a situation in which you have experienced this emotion with some intensity. When you have the situation firmly in mind, notice how this feeling manifests itself in your body. Remember, the purpose of this exercise is to observe and learn information about yourself. Try not to judge the feeling or your body's response to it.

Repeat this exercise with the other three feelings. When you are finished, take a few minutes to be one with everything you experienced. With your eyes still closed, notice the body sensations that came up as you focused on each feeling. When you are ready, open your eyes and use the four questions below as a guide for greater clarification:

1. What was the most interesting thing I learned?

2. What surprised me the most?

3. What did I already know about my body that was confirmed during this imagery?

4. What did I learn about my body that I did not know?

As you go about your daily life, try to tune in to your feelings. Notice how you experience them in your body. Over time, you will become more skilled at associating your body sensations with your emotions. As you do, and the emotional messages are revealed, the feelings often subside and even disappear.

CHAPTER 3

Emotions Are Logical:
Scientific versus Emotional Logic

The simplicity of a children's story often illustrates a profound truth. For example, when the main character in Antoine de Saint-Exupery's classic tale *The Little Prince* travels the world, he meets a wise fox that teaches him important lessons. As they get ready to part company, the fox offers the Little Prince his most valued secret: "It is only with the heart that one sees rightly; what is essential is invisible to the eye." It is a secret that the little prince remembers and treasures.

This message has many important implications, especially for your emotional well-being. Understanding your feelings is essential for a happy, balanced life, but since emotions are "invisible to the eye," they are often thought of as insignificant. You can witness the *effects* of feelings, such as items broken during a temper tantrum (anger) or tears after being rejected (sadness), but you cannot actually measure the feelings of anger or sadness in the same way you measure what you see, such as the height of a table or width of a chair. Emotions are generally viewed as inconsequential, frequently appearing as annoying intruders at the most inappropriate times. As discussed in chapter 2, feelings are often perceived as something to be eliminated as quickly and efficiently as possible.

You may think that emotions are illogical and have minimal influence on your decisions. However, paradoxically, the opposite is true. *Feelings have their own logic system,* and it is emotional, *not* scientific, logic that dictates your perceptions and decisions! Therefore, in this chapter we'll compare and contrast the scientific and emotional logic paradigms, as well as their healing potentials. Within each paradigm we'll look at Basic Principles and at Healing Strategies, followed by a case history to illustrate these principles.

Scientific Logic

Basic Principles

The general perception of the world is based on a scientific structure. This model, in turn, provides a logic system that *appears* to govern reality. Scientific logic is most easily explained as a framework where principles are defined by the five senses. This means that most of us distinguish our reality based on what we can touch, taste, feel, see, or smell. Scientific logic emanates from the portion of the brain known as the *cortex.* This area is where the logic we are familiar with resides. It is the home of our reflective processes such as problem solving, self-awareness, speech, and all other areas related to higher consciousness. As human beings, we are very comfortable identifying with the tasks and logic that originate in the cortex.

This scientific paradigm is greatly respected, and rightfully so. The findings from this model have physically and materially improved our quality of living, from astonishing medical breakthroughs to a spectrum of extraordinary inventions. There is strong emphasis on instruction within this logic system, ranging from formal learning in schools to manuals explaining the latest electronic devices. In essence, we *expect* to be educated and trained; otherwise, these concepts and gadgets seem incomplete and useless.

Healing Strategies

From a scientific perspective, *healing* is defined in the *American Heritage Dictionary* as "to restore to health, or soundness; cure." In this model, the definition implies *elimination* of the symptom. For example, when we have a severe sore throat or cough, a physician is likely to prescribe medication and send us home. Often the symptom is gone after a relatively short time, and the inference thus is that we have become well, or "fixed," by eliminating the symptom. However, the underlying cause of the condition may remain.

Emotional Logic

Basic Principles

In truth, emotions are also logical, but you may presently lack the information and skills needed to understand this powerful resource. Emotional logic is almost the antithesis of its scientific counterpart. As previously stated, emotions are neither seen nor valued, so it may be difficult to believe that there are specific methods to explain their significant messages. According to our cultural norms, you are "supposed to know" how to handle your feelings by observing those around you, since emotions are not equated with the need to learn. In actuality, emotions *are* logical and *do* require skills to be deciphered and understood.

The emotional logic system is housed in what is considered the more primitive portion of the brain, the *limbic system*. Unlike the cortex, which originates only in the human brain, the limbic system is found in animals as well as humans. Since the limbic system is instinctual and primitive, you, as a human being, are not always comfortable identifying with its tasks. A primary and powerful limbic goal is survival. It becomes activated when animals or humans perceive any type of danger.

Humans and animals handle potential threats in much the same manner. In the animal kingdom, when an unfamiliar animal approaches, an assessment is made based on nonverbal, instinctual information housed in the limbic system. For instance, if a wolf approaches a deer, judgments are made by each animal to help decide whether the other is friend, foe, or lunch! In humans, when unfamiliar people are introduced, you scan the strangers by assessing their verbal behaviors and—even more so—their nonverbal ones, such as their body language or tone of voice. These behavioral interpretations are commonly referred to as "vibes." Based on instinct and prior experience, they also originate in the limbic system.

In situations where you have no choice but to be in the company of the new arrival, you still make judgments about how to best handle the individual based on these principles. In other words, you evaluate exactly what is a safe and comfortable distance away from the other person, and you assess how much you want to interact with that individual.

With animals or humans, the reaction to a perceived threat is manifested in one of the following ways: fight, flight, freeze, or follow. These four reactions are commonly grouped together and referred to as the fight-or-flight response. Among humans as well as animals, all reactions to perceived danger can be reduced to one of these four, although human reactions often are more veiled than those among animals facing threats. For example, a human's fight response does not necessarily involve a physical encounter or the use of an object as a weapon. Instead, words are often the weapon of choice, and they can be destructive or even deadly. Fleeing, among humans, may denote not only physically leaving the scene of perceived danger but also mentally fleeing by denying a situation or attempting to distract the attacker. Distraction occurs when someone uses denial or humor or deflects the threat by presenting unrelated information. Freezing, for humans, can mean either standing still or doing nothing about the threat and thereby ignoring its potential destructiveness. Following or submitting, which broadly signifies giving in or surrendering to whatever is the perceived danger, does not necessarily involve the loss of one's life, for a human, although that could be an outcome. Instead, it may entail giving in to the demands or requests of the other, the source of the perceived threat. All of these human calculations may happen on a conscious level, but they are more likely to occur unconsciously.

Sigmund Freud, a pioneer in psychology, noted more than a century ago that emotional behavior is linked to the limbic system. He emphasized *the power and importance of emotions in unconsciously dictating actions and choices.* Recent research has proven him correct. A *Newsweek* article in 2002 titled "What Freud Got Right" stated:

> The key to understanding his theory is that these were unconscious drives shaping our behavior without the mediation of our waking minds.... Researchers have found evidence that Freud's drives really do exist, and they have their roots in the limbic system, a primitive part of the brain that operates mostly below the horizon of consciousness. Now more commonly referred to as emotions, the modern suite of drives comprises five: rage, panic, separation, distress, lust and a variation on libido sometimes called seeking.

Healing Strategies

Emotional healing operates from a different paradigm than its scientific counterpart. In this perspective, healing is about *managing* feelings, not eliminating them. It is virtually impossible to eradicate the effect of early negative responses from caretakers, since their reactions were hammered into our being daily. Children's response to this pounding is generally denial and repression. In turn, their unexpressed emotions become tightly embedded within their psyches, capturing the youngsters in a viselike grip.

It is easy to understand why eliminating feelings seems to be the answer. It is closely related to your strong desire to make the unhappy situation go away. Many people in distress spend huge sums of time and money pursuing this illusory goal. Desperately wanting to "get rid of" whatever is troubling them, clients almost always initially request that I help fix or eliminate their issues. One of my first responsibilities is to explain that true and lasting emotional healing involves beginning to accept, rather than seeking to eliminate, whatever is troubling them—*no matter what their issues may be*. Self-acceptance is the only means of ending the raging intrapsychic war of self-blame and negative thinking. Once you can *begin* to accept the truth, you can embark on the healing process. As discussed in chapter 6, achieving this goal is not necessarily difficult, but doing so requires commitment and a true desire for change.

Illustrating Scientific versus Emotional Logic: Suzanna

Suzanna was a bright, successful thirty-four-year-old professional and divorced mother of three-year-old Janette. Suzanna was a survivor of repeated sexual abuse by an older brother, but she firmly believed these painful memories were over. She came to my office to resolve what she perceived as a separate issue. Although she was on a tight budget, she found herself compelled to buy almost everything in toy stores for Janette. This seemed illogical, since Janette generally made few requests. Suzanna's debt had accumulated rapidly over the past year, and yet she felt compelled to continue. In essence, she felt driven and out of control. The compulsion to spend money on her daughter was becoming very costly, both monetarily and emotionally.

During our first few sessions, Suzanna spent most of the time talking. She needed to share everything regarding her increasing debt. After hearing her concerns, I asked if she was willing to do some experiential work to unlock the dilemma. She agreed, and I chose a simple body-mind exercise. I then instructed her to formulate a sentence that would best describe her predicament. Suzanna quickly replied, "I can't stop spending money, particularly on Janette." I asked her to repeat the sentence a few times and notice what was happening in her body. Suzanne quickly reported a tightening and a nauseous feeing in her stomach, and she became visibly shaken. I then had her identify the feelings that the physical sensations were attempting to express. Suzanna quickly responded and named fear. I suggested she close her eyes and imagine surrounding both the sensation and the feeling with a protective light. We then did the Healing Breath exercise described at the end of chapter 1. At the completion of the exercise, I explained that these sensations and feelings were messengers from her emotional world. They were either trying to protect her, remind her, or teach her something. I advised her to communicate with her inner world to understand their meaning.

At first she did not connect to any awareness, and then suddenly, she opened her eyes and her mouth dropped open. "My goodness, I can't believe what I just saw." Suzanna spoke about seeing an image of being raped by her brother. A torrent of emotions surfaced, and we spent time allowing her to release and process these feelings. She said she was shocked, since she perceived being at peace with the events. As Suzanna received comfort, validation, and support for her flood of emotions, she eventually was able to calm down and refocus. I gently asked her if she could make a connection between the sentence she had formed earlier and the feelings that had surfaced. Suzanna understood that they were somehow related, but she was too overwhelmed to make a connection.

I suggested we do the Healing Breath again, and she agreed. Following the exercise, she appeared more relaxed. I asked the question about connection once more. This time her face responded with a look of horror. What came to her awareness was a profound unconscious association. Suzanna understood the absolute necessity to anticipate and buy everything for Janette. She feared that if she did not, the youngster would want something and have to look to another adult to satisfy that need. The price for her daughter, her deep terror revealed, might be sexual in nature. It took many sessions to integrate this awareness she thought had long been forgotten. Once she worked it through on a deeper level, Suzanna was able to translate her awareness into new behaviors. This shift resulted in her ability to use more discretion in spending money, especially with regard to Janette.

This case example powerfully illustrates the differences between scientific and emotional logic. Suzanna was aware that her focus *should* be on paying off the debt. In her *thoughts*, Suzanna *knew* she should not continue spending more money, although she felt compelled to do so. However true her thoughts and "shoulds" were, they were intellectual assumptions originating from scientific logic. As we can see, this logic is deemed powerless when a perceived threat to survival is at stake, because this threat is the *primary* fear for all living beings. In Suzanna's case, the unconscious menace was the dangerous possibility of a sexual encounter for Janette in exchange for something her daughter might want. When viewed from the perspective of emotional logic, Suzanna's behaviors, as well as the behaviors of others, begin to make more sense.

Before proceeding, two more facts about the limbic system and emotional logic need to be mentioned.

Early trauma is stored in the limbic system. However, the limbic system does not have the ability to use words, since speech originates in the cortex.

The limbic system's lack of language is critical to remember, because it implies that you need both nonverbal and verbal tools for true healing to occur. Nonverbal exercises, such as guided imagery, hypnosis, EMDR, or body-mind work, serve to safely access issues on the *same experiential nonverbal level* where the emotional wounding originally occurred. However, as mentioned previously, this aspect of healing needs to take place with a professional. In Suzanna's example, cognitive awareness was not sufficient for lasting change. Her case reflected this truth, because she knew the "right thing to do" (based in the cortex) but found herself compelled to act in what appeared to be a potentially destructive manner (based in the limbic system). Suzanna's emotional healing had not taken place because the heart of the issue had not been addressed. In other words, she had not dealt with the root cause of the issue—namely, her fear masked deeper feelings of anger, betrayal, and sadness.

Suzanna's example clearly demonstrates the importance of reexamining frustrations from an emotional perspective. If that reexamination does not happen, the negative thought "I should know better" may not be the whole truth. Unfortunately, none of us come with manuals at birth explaining how we operate!

The limbic system has no sense of time.

The primitive portion of the brain cannot distinguish whether a traumatic event occurred in your childhood or yesterday. In other words, the limbic system views events from a timeless perspective. Therefore, the unconscious portion of the brain often perceives a stimulus as threatening in the present, when in fact it may not be dangerous. The perceived threat is linked to childhood memories and not necessarily the present reality. This truth becomes apparent in the following abbreviated case illustration.

Overreacting and the Limbic System: Joe

Joe, age forty-two, experienced childhood abandonment by his mother. Since this wounding had not been properly addressed, Joe's abandonment issue still played havoc in his life, specifically in his intense negative response to lateness. From the scientific perspective, being ten minutes late may be perceived as a minor infraction, but he experienced it as a devastating blow. Even though the wounding had happened decades earlier, he reacted with what appeared to be a disproportionate degree of emotions such as anger, fear, and sadness. He had temper tantrums and used profanity to vent his pent-up feelings.

Since the limbic portion of the brain is timeless, Joe remained unaware that the original stimulus of abandonment no longer applied. He was incapable of understanding the significance of his overreactions and viewed the other person as being totally at fault. Over time, this behavior cost him a number of significant relationships. In truth, Joe's response was merely his primitive warning signal that a threat (abandonment) might be imminent. Thus, what appears as illogical on one level (scientific) makes perfect sense on another (emotional). As stated earlier, Freud's alternative name for these responses from the limbic system is "unconscious reactions."

Does the scientific logic system ever prevail? It does indeed. It can perform when, and only when, the emotional world perceives no viable sense of danger, or, in other words, when a sense of safety is felt. When emotional safety appears to be ensured, the higher functions of the cortex and scientific logic become feasible. Only then can the use of scientific logic and creativity become possible to solve problems. It is also the time when personal awareness and inner growth are likely to occur. However, at *any* sign of perceived threat to either animal or human, scientific logic disappears and the quest for survival prevails.

Disconnection from emotional logic is a major contributor to your confusion about feelings. Now it is time to learn the skills to decipher the valuable messages of your emotions. The next chapter contains the guidance for you to do just that.

Testing the Power of the Limbic System

Think about yourself and reflect on how you respond to a perceived physical or verbal attack. For example:

- Do you strike back verbally or physically (fight)?
- Do you run away or attempt to distract the attacker (flight)?
- Do you deny the situation, become immobilized, and do nothing (freeze)?
- Do you generally do what the attacker has requested (follow)?

Notice how your responses to a perceived attack can be reduced to fit into one of four categories discussed in this chapter: fight, flight, freeze, or follow.

Now that you have thought about these reactions during this exercise, you may find it helpful to observe your responses to a potential perceived attack during the coming week. Notice whether you tend to respond with one particular reaction overall or whether your responses vary, based on the person or situation. By identifying the patterns of the memories, feelings, and images that are evoked by these particular reactions, you will gain greater insight into yourself.

You may find it helpful to journal about what you have learned.

Note: If it does not feel comfortable to think about yourself for this exercise, pick someone else you know well.

CHAPTER 4

Emotional Messages: Why They Hide and How They Can Help

F ew of us escape psychological wounding; it is inevitable. As adults, we try desperately to disguise our pain. We become almost obsessive about seeing who can hide it best and appear "the most together." However, as hard as we try, it is virtually impossible to conceal. As discussed in chapter 2, the pain eventually seeps through as you feel more disconnected from yourself and as a result, you long for connection to others. Thus, a significant addiction emerges of being accepted and valued by the outside world, often at the expense of yourself and your needs. This craving for others' approval stems from poor self-worth and the erroneous feelings that you are defective and not enough. A related mistaken belief is that achieving others' good opinion can be accomplished by accumulating possessions. Material acquisitions represent the external symbol of power and status. This type of wealth is often associated with social approval. This external pursuit, although deceptive, is alluring, and it provides both intensity and diversion from our internal issues. However, it is very important to remember that this quest has no correlation to a sense of *inner* empowerment and self-value.

The pursuit of material acquisition often results in being seduced by adrenaline, a hormone controlled by the limbic system. Adrenaline release is a physiological response to stress. When

41

discharged into the body, adrenaline causes a reaction that has been described as a "rush" or "high." Since the release of adrenaline can be perceived as exciting and pleasurable, the sensations often become a source of unconscious addiction. In this example, the fear of not being accepted by others, which in the limbic system represents a threat to survival, is the stimulus that causes the release of adrenaline. The sensation of the rush signifies to the primitive brain that a reaction to the threat has been unleashed. A problem arises if you fail to recognize that the true source of the rush—namely, fear for your survival—and, instead, associate the rush with your efforts to gain status, approval, and material possessions.

In addition, the road to material accomplishment proclaims to the world, "Look at me! See, I really am okay!" The more you achieve, the more "okay" you perceive yourself to be. You falsely believe that being "okay" means being accepted and valued by others. It is an unconscious protection you feel will insulate you from rejection and despair. Your pursuit is generally blinding. If you finally achieve what you have so long desired, you often say, "Is that all there is?"

Why do you run from yourself with such passion? Why do you allow your perceived demons to remain hidden and yet rule you with an iron hand? The answer is that, even as a competent adult, you unconsciously perceive yourself to be incapable of combating your early traumas. You recognize your pain as menacing and believe yourself to be in a battle that is certain to be lost. It is as if you hear the sounds of distant trumpets echoing your downfall. Thus, your wounds remain buried, and, paradoxically, so do your chances for healing.

The disempowerment of these *perceived* demons—in reality, helpful messengers in disguise—begins when you embark on a healing journey. To do this you must accomplish three important tasks: be receptive to change; realize you can sabotage your growth by ignoring emotional messages, especially those of fear, sadness, and anger; and recognize the importance of deciphering your feelings' valuable communications.

Be receptive to change.

Effectively handling old traumas implies a shift that requires changing your perceptions and behaviors. This is not easy. Change is viewed as uncertain and frightening, while the status quo is safe and familiar. Therefore, you generally opt for what is known. Such choices are made even if the outcome keeps you trapped in negative dynamics. Rather than creating an honest relationship with yourself, you turn away from signals that warn of destructive behaviors. You are unwilling to take the leap of faith that change requires. However, until you do, you will remain helpless and miserable.

Realize that you sabotage your growth by ignoring your emotional messages, especially those of fear, sadness, and anger.

The significance of not decoding your feelings results in an important outcome. It keeps you stuck and interferes with exploring positive alternatives. Although all emotions have valuable information, three basic feelings are the most frequently ignored and, paradoxically, offer the most significant guidance: fear, sadness, and anger. The one probably disregarded most is fear. It represents a powerful force in most of our lives because of its primitive association with life and death. When you feel fear, you think it is an indicator to avoid the person or situation that frightens you. *In truth, fear is simply a signal of caution.* You only need to apply its meaning to your particular situation. The message can encourage some type of perceptual shift and/or behavioral change. Once you understand the meaning of fear's message, any situation can be handled more productively. Fear, as well as the other feeling categories, is described in greater detail later in the chapter.

43

Recognize the importance of deciphering emotional messages.

In the process of decoding your feelings, you need to realize that all feelings can be placed into five basic groups of emotions: *anger, fear, sadness, joy,* and *sexuality.* These are similar to the unconscious drives cited by researchers in the *Newsweek* article titled "What Freud Got Right" (discussed in chapter 3). In this article they are referred to as rage (anger), panic (fear), separation (sadness), a variation of the libido sometimes called seeking (joy), and lust (sexuality).

As indicated in the following list, each of the five feelings ranges in intensity. Each feeling is associated with specific emotional messages and with manifestations in certain body areas. You can explore your own personal associations and compare them with the listed ones by revisiting the exercise at the end of chapter 2.

Feeling Categories

With each of the five feelings, the range is described in terms of the mildest to the most extreme degree to which someone might experience the feeling. For any given emotion, most people have experienced a broad series of intensities, even if only momentarily.

Anger: The range includes feeling annoyed, frustrated, infuriated, or uncontrollably enraged. *Anger communicates the message of physical or psychological violation, betrayal, and/or disrespect.* Anger is often expressed physically in the neck, jaw, and shoulders. Symptoms such as a stiff neck, jaw constriction, and tight shoulders are examples of anger manifesting in the body.

Sadness: The range includes feeling disappointed, misunderstood, hurt, depressed, lonely, or abandoned. *Sadness communicates the message of some type of psychological or physical loss.* Sadness is physically associated with the midline area from the throat to the belly. Symptoms such as a lump in the throat, tightness in the chest, and queasiness in the stomach are examples of sadness manifesting in the body.

Fear: The range includes feeling scared, intimidated, frightened, or overwhelmingly terrified. *Fear communicates the message of a physical or psychological threat to survival.* The threat of physical survival can mean destruction or death; the threat to psychological survival may signify the loss of a job, a relationship, or health. Symptoms such as jitters or butterflies in the stomach, sweaty palms, rapid heartbeat, or a nauseous sensation are examples of fear manifesting in the body.

Joy: The range includes feeling physically and psychologically happy, content, or serene and peaceful. *Joy is related to a sense of safety.* A feeling of being safe and, subsequently, joyful becomes possible when you release your vigilance against fear, anger, or sadness. When you feel safe and joyful, your energy can be directed to more pleasurable activities such as play, nurturance, rest, and sex. Joy is physically associated with muscle relaxation and a sense of peace. *Only* when you feel a sense of safety are you likely to experiment with new behaviors.

Sexuality: The range includes feeling attracted, excited, or physically stimulated. *Sexuality communicates the message of physical connection.* Sexuality is often experienced in proximity to the sexual organs.

The following client examples demonstrate the powerful significance and healing potential of emotional messages.

Deciphering the Message of Fear: Jill

Jill, a single woman in her mid-thirties, came to my office aware that she had a deep fear of abandonment. She reported a recent sense of overall anxiety, although she could not understand why. The only thing that had recently changed was that her partner of six months, Mark, wanted to modify the parameters of their relationship. Although he still desired to see her, Mark wanted to decrease the time they spent together. Jill was very happy with Mark and cited all the "logical reasons" why his decision was acceptable. However, I detected conflicting bodily messages. I noted overall body tension and increased speed in her speech pattern when she discussed her partner.

After doing some Emotional Wisdom experiential work, her deeper truth emerged. Jill became aware that, despite what she said, she was terrified about losing Mark. She also learned that the message of fear was merely an archaic *warning* of potential abandonment and did not guarantee rejection. Jill recognized that she had options: she could modify, accept, or reject the agreement. Her new understanding resulted in tremendous relief. She became aware that she could explore action steps for compromise based on both partners' needs. Also, Jill acknowledged that if compromise proved impossible, the relationship would not meet *her* needs and therefore might require *her* reconsideration. This information and her potential action plan were empowering. As a result, she left the session feeling dramatically relieved and more at peace.

As stated earlier, many people also tend to ignore the emotionally potent messages of anger and sadness. *The message of anger is a perception of being violated or betrayed, either physically or psychologically; the message of sadness is a perception of loss, either physically or psychologically.* Ignoring their meanings can interfere with change and can arise for various reasons. For instance, you may unconsciously perceive your own efforts to grow as ruptures of an old, unspoken childhood agreement—namely, your caretakers would give you the love necessary for survival only if you would surrender your authentic self to them. Given such a perception, you may now unconsciously believe that, to survive, you fully relinquished yourself long ago and that once in a lifetime should be enough!

Most likely, you move into adulthood unaware that you carry such an implicit conviction. However, life inevitably will present you with circumstances—usually related to some type of loss—that will challenge your inertia. In order to deal with these circumstances, you often will have to change, and this necessity may make you feel angry and sad. You may say, "This is not the way it is supposed to be!" The profound paradox is that only when you know *your truth*—no matter what that might be, in terms of your past experiences and your current beliefs—can inner peace be possible. The case history of Maria illustrates this principle.

Recognizing Unconscious Childhood Contracts: Maria

Maria, a bright, shy, single female in her mid-forties, began Emotional Wisdom work after having been in previous therapy. She reported that she had some understanding of her issues, but the awareness had produced no behavioral change. Maria described herself as irresponsible and childlike. Although she worked and lived alone, she portrayed herself as psychologically dependent on her aging parents.

We began our work by having her formulate a single sentence that best expressed her frustration. The sentence Maria chose was "I feel stuck." After she repeated the sentence numerous times, I asked if she could associate it with any feelings. At first she hesitated and then described fear and anger. As mentioned earlier, fear is an indicator of *a perceived threat to survival,* and anger is *a perceived threat of being violated or disrespected.* When I questioned her on how these feelings might relate to her sentence, her response was a blank look.

After a few seconds, however, her facial expression registered what I interpreted as shock. She took a breath and replied, "Oh, my goodness! If I became unstuck, my parents would have no reason to stay alive. My remaining dependent gives them a focus and keeps them going. Being empowered would mean I could take care of myself and finally grow up. This would be a sign that they are no longer needed!" Thus, from Maria's emotional logic, becoming unstuck was completely terrifying. To her, growing up meant that she might abandon her parents and thereby cause them to die.

Maria's profound fear also illustrated her resistance to taking responsibility for her choices. As part of the unconscious contract Maria had with her parents, she unwittingly allowed her parents to reinforce her childlike behaviors as a *perceived* tradeoff for being cared for by them. As a result, her parents did not encourage her to develop the skills necessary to become a fully functioning adult. The realizations that emerged were a complete shock to Maria and began to uproot an old belief system. We spent many subsequent sessions processing the ramifications. Presently, we are working on creating a sense of safety for Maria by developing small action steps. These steps will provide a path toward greater independence.

Clearly, emotions contain valuable information that can guide you toward inner awareness and a sense of peace—reason enough to learn skills to decipher their meanings. However, just in case you still have any doubts about the significance of these powerful tools, consider the following facts.

Although words are important and necessary vehicles of communication, they can separate us from our authentic self.

Words serve as a source of connection as well as separation. They connect one human being to another, because words are a vehicle of communication. As Neale Donald Walsch, author and international speaker, in *Conversations with God*, states, "Words may help you to understand something." However, they are also a source of separation, since the words you use frequently do not communicate your deepest truth. You often get unconsciously entangled in the web words create. As Walsch states, "Words are merely utterances and noises that stand for feelings, thoughts and experience. Signs. Insignias. They are not the Truth. They are not the real thing. ...Words are the least purveyor of Truth."

It is through *your feelings* that your authenticity is expressed. This fact is demonstrated in the case histories presented throughout the book, including the two examples discussed in this chapter. In the first instance, Jill came into the session stating that she was fine with Mark's decision to spend less time together. In truth, she was simply rationalizing and denying her genuine feeling: fear of abandonment. In the second example, Maria chose to live with the misery of being stuck, rather than face her real message: she unconsciously feared her truth would kill her parents. In both examples, the clients needed to be released from the grip of their illusions. These realizations led to shifts in perception, development of action plans, and ultimately, greater peace.

Below every powerful thought are feelings. These emotions represent your true inner messengers; they are always trying to guide you in a positive direction.

In *Conversations with God*, Walsch says, "Feelings are the language of the soul...Hidden in your deepest feeling is your highest truth…If you want to know what's true for you about something, look at how you're *feeling* about it…The trick is to get to those feelings." In essence, that is the goal of the Emotional Wisdom process.

As discussed earlier, feelings often appear at first glance to be "negative," but that is a superficial interpretation. In actuality, emotional messages are always giving you positive guidance, and it is merely their primitive nature that produces this perception. Although often appearing in a frightening disguise, they are simply attempting to direct you to a more fulfilling solution to *any* of life's issues. *Feelings are your true friends and the keepers of valuable knowledge.* The Emotional Wisdom process and the insights presented in this book are designed to help you interpret these messages and positively reframe the problem at hand.

Emotional messages are always trying to provide helpful guidance, even if you initially experience them as uncomfortable.

You need to remember that feelings are housed in the limbic system, the most primitive part of the brain, and therefore communicate in archaic and cryptic ways. As a result, you often are unfamiliar and uneasy with the discomfort of these messages. If you remain unaware that these primal signals are the only means available to the limbic system for conveying their wisdom, you will not recognize emotions as *indicators* of what you need to know. Instead, as demonstrated in the client examples, you will do your best to suppress and ignore them.

It is very common to confuse thoughts with feelings.

When you think of emotions, you may tend to associate a wide range of experiences that are complex and at times indefinable, leading to expressions of your perceptions or thoughts when you actually intended to articulate your emotions. To help clarify the distinction, let us suppose you say to someone, "I feel like you don't understand!" The thought expressed in this statement has its origins in the cortex, or logical portion of the brain. It signifies the idea that what you are saying is not comprehended or appreciated by another. The thought, however, does not acknowledge *hidden feelings* that are likely to be evoked. These emotions, which are housed in the limbic system, express your deeper truths and rule your responses. The hidden feelings likely include sadness, anger, and most significantly, fear. You are not consciously withholding these feelings; generally you are not aware of the deeper truth.

Using the previous sentence, let us examine the underlying emotional messages. The sentence was, "I feel like you don't understand!" As stated earlier, the feelings accompanying this thought are often anger, sadness, and fear. Remember, the message of anger is about disrespect or betrayal, and it evokes the feeling that you are being disrespected by another for not understanding your point of view. Sadness is a message related to loss, and in this instance it is about the loss of your ideas being understood. The powerful feeling of fear is associated with the message of a perceived threat to survival—in this instance, a psychological threat to your existence or the survival of the relationship. It is no wonder that you become angry, sad, and afraid!

However, irrespective of what you say to defend yourself, you are likely to be unconsciously terrified that something within you is flawed. You fear that being unable to express yourself successfully signifies that *you are defective*. From the perspective of the primitive brain that houses your emotions, if you are defective, you can easily be rejected or abandoned. The potential of being abandoned can emotionally imply the possibility of psychological death (yours or the relationship with the person who did not understand you). Thus, a simple thought masks a host of emotional meanings.

Since both humans and animals have a limbic system, the underlying terror of abandonment and ultimate death can be witnessed in animals as well. In the animal kingdom, if one being is perceived by others as defective, the animal is generally abandoned for the survival of the herd. It becomes cumbersome and even dangerous to modify the pack's behavior to the needs of one of its members, because doing so would make them more vulnerable to attack and death. In most cases, even the mother recognizes the necessity of such desertion and will forsake her young. This abandonment leaves the animal at the mercy of assault, starvation, and eventual death. It is this precise pattern of feeling and behavior that happens unconsciously on the human level when we are confronted with potential abandonment.

Emotional interpretations are based on two scenarios.

One scenario that emotional interpretations may be based on occurs in your internal world and results in a personal interpretation of the event. Due to its individual associations, the interpretation is unlikely to be experienced by the others present. The following brief case example illustrates this concept.

Scenario 1: Personal Interpretation

Interpreting Events Based on Emotional Experience: Antoinette

A thirty-five year old woman, Antoinette, experienced a traumatic childhood incident in a room where the only object present was a huge spider plant. The plant unconsciously became associated in Antoinette's mind with the disturbing occurrence. Years later, when she walked into a room that had a similar-looking plant, she experienced some of the same unconscious feelings of that horrific event. Other people in the room did not have a similar reaction and could not understand what appeared to be

Antoinette's unprovoked, exaggerated response. In her reality, the plant was an archaic trigger that evoked the original traumatic event, and she momentarily relived those feelings as if the event were actually recurring.

Scenario 2: General Consensus

The second scenario is an incident that occurs in the external world and is observable by all, resulting in a consensual interpretation of the event. An example of an observable event would be if someone walked into a room with a loaded gun. Everyone witnessing the event would likely feel some form of fear. Thus, those present would have the same reference point for terror, and there would be group consensus. This is unlike Antoinette's experience, where she alone had the association that produced panic.

The key point to remember from both scenarios is that *all emotional interpretations are meaningful and valid.* This is significant because it is common to deny feelings that are not concretely associated with one of the five senses and validated by other people.

However, you may not truly feel connected to your own emotions—until you have worked through more of the exercises in this book. In the following exercise, you can reexamine some of your experiences through the lens of Emotional Wisdom and, perhaps, understand your underlying feelings more clearly.

Decoding Your Feelings

To understand how deciphering your feelings works, take one experience you have had with each of the five feelings. To start, it will be easier if you take an incident that you would not consider too significant. Using each feeling one at a time, answer each of the following questions:

1. The feeling I have selected is _____. (Chose *one at a time* from the following: anger, sadness, fear, joy, or sexuality). Describe the incident that illustrates the feeling you have selected:

   _____

   _____

   _____

   _____

2. Apply the *message* of the feeling you have chosen for the incident.

   _____

   _____

   _____

   _____

3. Explore what has been revealed to you about the deeper truth of your situation.

   _____

   _____

   _____

   _____

After having completed the exercise, give yourself some time to reflect on what came to mind as you applied each feeling and deciphered each message. Do not be surprised if you find that the process, although perhaps awkward at first, is a relatively quick tool to enhance your awareness of your deeper truth. Keep the practice in mind and apply it when you desire clarity.

The Healing Process

CHAPTER 5

Myths That Trap Us
and Truths That Free Us

Exploring the three phases of emotional healing will be clearer if you first understand three prevalent myths that discourage you from choosing to heal. This chapter briefly explores each of them, as well as the truths that can free you, and concludes with a client example that illustrates both.

Myth 1: *If I really want to heal, I must take an honest look at myself, which means I will have to assume self-blame for making things such a mess!*

It is true that to positively change, you have to explore the various reasons your life is not where you would like it to be. This requires self-discovery, which sadly is often inhibited by two factors. The first, discussed in chapter 2, is feeling unsafe about acknowledging or expressing emotions. The second is our cultural style of teaching. Although there is a strong *intellectual* emphasis on positive reinforcement, in reality, correction generally occurs through negative comments. Examples of such remarks in both family and formal settings include, "I told you not to try that," "How could you have done that?" and "What's the matter with you?" Eventually, you internalize these statements and no longer need the presence of someone to evoke them; they "play" automatically in your head. As a result, the implicit message "It's your fault!" resonates loudly, threatening the quest for your authentic self. The danger is based on the fear that self-exploration will justify your inner blame. So you remain trapped and hopeless in a vortex of turbulent feelings that you unconsciously avoid at any cost.

You remain unaware that, since childhood, blame is a mirror of the insecurity experienced by the adults in your world. This well-hidden truth generally results from two experiences. First, the adult likely received negative reinforcement in his or her early life, and it became a familiar, unconscious tool passed along to the child. Second, teachers or parents often experience a deep, unconscious fear of *their own defectiveness and inadequacy* about instructing or correcting a youngster. The negativity is a way of hiding that insecurity from the child, as well as themselves.

Truth 1: *If I really want to heal, I need to congratulate myself for having the courage and strength to face my issues.*

Although well worth the time and energy, the healing journey requires courage as well as strength. Courage is essential, since healing is often met with resistance from those closest to us. This resistance occurs because others have an unconscious investment in maintaining the status quo. The investment is an assurance that they will not be forced to look at *their* issues, which is always a threat if a significant other is in the process of change. You are given a multitude of subtle and not-so-subtle messages to discourage and shame you into remaining with the status quo. If you allow this to happen, you will continue to feel victimized, helpless, and miserable.

The process of Emotional Wisdom, however, has no room for self-blame. From this paradigm, everything is a learning process—no matter how horrendous or unspeakable you *perceive* your issues to be. If you can learn from your history, you will be on the path to freedom. This liberation occurs not because the original dynamics are gone but because your reactions change. Your responses will be fortified with awareness, compassion, and above all, choice.

In fact, congratulations are in order, because taking this step toward healing is a genuine demonstration of emotional strength. This form of strength is frequently unacknowledged, since we tend to identify strength from the model of scientific logic. According to this paradigm, strength is a measurable form of physical prowess evidenced by warding off a physical threat, excelling in a competitive arena, and so on. In this model, strength is generally rewarded by material possessions and monetary wealth; therefore, strength is perceived as power.

In Emotional Wisdom, which embraces emotional logic, strength derives from an internal resource. Since such strength is not directly measurable, it is often not subject to the same rewards as its scientific counterpart. Inner strength basically originates from one source: the willingness to let go of denial and admit that something is not right in your life. This, in essence, gives you the courage to face yourself and explore your emotional messages. Only then will you learn your *perceived* demons are merely disguises and in truth are pathways to valuable lessons. Such growth encourages a sense of internal peace. This tranquility serves as a powerful antidote to the never-ending, exhausting intrapsychic battle within us all. A true tribute to your internal strength is the willingness to do this even at the *perceived* cost of potential shame you may feel or others may project.

It takes strength to admit your frailties and struggles, especially since such disclosure is generally viewed as a sign of weakness and vulnerability. In turn, you erroneously believe that you will be helpless against potential adversaries if you surrender your defenses. However, the deeper emotional truth is that *your vulnerability is your strength*. It takes courage to speak your truth, share your deepest fears, and air the skeletons you have so desperately tried to conceal. It is only when you shine the light of awareness and acceptance on your issues that these internal demons recede and become virtually powerless.

The key is that you need to choose wisely with whom you share this precious process. The selection can include close friends, who can significantly contribute to your healing by providing validation, clarification, and reassuring acceptance. You may be fortunate to have friends who have the compassion, wisdom, and time to help you consistently process your issues. Nevertheless, friends—no matter how loyal and loving—do not have all the components available on a sustained basis, nor are they likely to have the expertise so necessary for portions of the healing journey. The essential reliability and knowledge required by the inner growth process indicate that you would be wise to seek a professional resource at some point. Choosing to do this is also associated with the next prevalent myth.

Myth 2: *I should be able to do this healing alone, and if I need support, it is an even greater sign to the world and to myself that there is something wrong with me.*

You may be well acquainted with this myth. The irony is that in other areas of life, you value training. For example, whenever you learn some type of physical or mechanical skills—ones needed for concrete, measurable activities—you rightfully expect to need instruction. However, in the world of unseen feelings, the common thinking is that emotions do not require education and should be manageable by observation. Society generally views problem solving as the ultimate answer to being able to cope emotionally. Although this step may be a later part of the process, it is first necessary to decipher and understand the messages your feelings are trying to convey.

Truth 2: *I recognize that guidance from another person can be an essential part of healing. In addition to awareness, the relationship with that person can allow me to experience unconditional acceptance. Feeling this deep, sustained approval might be entirely new to me.*

Healing requires a true acceptance. *The experience of compassion as a healing tool is a key antidote for persistent messages of shame.* Without such acceptance, it is impossible to have compassion for your past. As psychiatrist Theodore Isaac Rubin states in his book *Compassion and Self-Hate*:

> I have found that human efforts, struggles, and insights (and I include psychoanalytic insights) are at best intellectual, superficial, and of minimal value without compassion…Compassion is the strongest human therapeutic agent in existence. Its potential for constructive growth and human creative possibility is almost endless.

Although essential for true change, self-acceptance is virtually impossible because most of us have been raised without any concept of what this means. You can most fully understand self-compassion by experiencing others' compassion toward you. Since your caretakers generally have not experienced empathy in their lives, they are unlikely to provide you with what is unfamiliar to them. However, receiving such compassion from other sources is possible no matter how horrendous or unspeakable you perceive your issues to be.

Sometimes the person offering this gift is a therapist, a good friend, or a teacher. What matters is not so much who the person is but whether the other's acceptance is honest and unconditional. As Jack Kornfield, clinical psychologist and Buddhist teacher, states so eloquently in *A Path with Heart*:

The process of inner healing inevitably requires developing a committed relationship with a teacher or guide. Because many of our greatest pains come from past relationships, it is through our experience of a wise and conscious relationship that these pains are healed. This relationship itself becomes the ground for our opening to compassion and freedom of the spirit. Where the pain and disappointment of the past have left us isolated and closed, with a wise teacher we can learn to trust again. When we allow our darkest fears and worst dimensions to be witnessed and compassionately accepted by another, we learn to accept them ourselves.

With self-acceptance, all things are possible. This includes your ability to heal issues that negatively impact your present and, in all probability, your future.

Myth 3: *If I begin the Emotional Wisdom process, the people I love will abandon me and I will be alone.*

As previously discussed, your personal growth may be viewed by others as an unconscious threat. Therefore, if you embark on a healing process, close relationships may be modified or eliminated. This shift is generally initiated by the client, but it can also originate from a significant family member or friend. Remembering that even a positive change is perceived—by you and others—to be scary, this myth can act as a powerful deterrent to growth.

On the other hand, even as a result of completing some healing work, you could initially feel compelled to continue relationships you perceive as harmful. If complex dynamics are involved, it is not always easy to immediately act upon what you have learned. Becoming aware does not mean you have to change things suddenly; it simply offers you a choice. The Emotional Wisdom approach provides you with options and supports your best interests in the reevaluation process.

Change is scary. In sharp contrast, the familiar offers predictability and comfort, irrespective of the anguish it may also harbor. Consider, for instance, the widely reported story of a child who was repeatedly abused by his mother and was temporarily removed from her home. Someone from a child protection agency took him to court so that the judge and jury could witness his many bruises, which were visibly black and blue. When he saw his mother, however, he cried out for her with open arms and clearly wanted to be with her. Obviously, his mother symbolized a familiar yet painful present, whereas the agency representative epitomized an uncertain future.

It is also important to know that when you are ready to change any relationship, the shift will be accompanied by a sense of loss, which is *completely* natural. A grief process evolves, even if you initiated the change. The unconscious is not aware that the choice was yours; it knows only that there now is an empty or modified space in your internal world. No matter how destructive the relationship and how much happier you are to be free, a natural void occurs. Being comfortable with life's many paradoxes is difficult, as is understanding how you can be happy to be rid of something that was truly not working and yet, simultaneously, feel sad. As previously stated, this seeming contradiction is to be expected.

Truth 3: *If I enter the Emotional Wisdom process, I recognize that I will be establishing a strong, enduring relationship with the most important person in my life—me! In addition, my healing will help me attract positive people, which will result in more satisfying relationships.*

Many of us are concerned with pleasing those around us, at our own expense. As discussed in chapter 2, this apprehension stems from the early messages that our survival depends on others' approval. We forget that once we become adults, we can and *should* shift the majority of that need for approval to ourselves. This is not to say we should not be a good member of society and cooperate with others; however, too many of us primarily focus our energies on pleasing others rather than balancing this effort with what *we* need and want.

Satisfying another person at your own expense is the origin of many difficulties. It makes you subject to the whims of others as you attempt to capture the affection you crave. In addition, you can never be sure when, at a moment's notice, you will be rejected, betrayed, or abandoned, leaving you crushed and confused. However, if you develop a relationship with yourself based on authenticity, you will be less likely to experience the same sense of loss. Because of your inner connection, you may be alone, but not lonely.

Being alone simply means being with yourself in an activity or in reflection and represents a loving acceptance of whatever you are feeling or doing at the time. However, you may unconsciously believe being alone signifies you are somehow lonely and defective. From this belief system, you erroneously assume self-blame because you are not able to be with someone who can offer you acceptance. Remember, however, that being in a bad relationship can be far lonelier than being on your own. As you heal, you will learn how to nurture and protect yourself, as well as when to be by yourself or with others. In essence, you will become your own best friend.

It is from this place of truth that you can decide what *you* need in relationships. As you shift, so do the types of people who enter your life. It is as if a space has been created for positive relationships that previously had been excluded unconsciously. Now, you welcome those people and relationships.

The following case example demonstrates how powerful these three myths are in influencing your perceptions and beliefs.

Identifying Myths That Trap Us: Jerry and Nance

Jerry and Nance came to my office for marital counseling. Jerry, in his mid- forties, was the tall, slim, well-dressed CEO of a successful manufacturing company. His wife, Nance, about the same age, was a well-groomed, attractive, full-time homemaker. Jerry very clearly stated that he was not happy to be in counseling, and his body language of crossed arms, tense posture, as well as furrowed brow affirmed his statement. He had consented to counseling only as a desperate last resort to save his marriage. His objection to therapy stemmed from his belief that this crisis was a private matter he and Nance should have been able to handle on their own (Myth 2).

He implied that being in a therapist's office was a reflection of his failure both as a partner and as a protector (Myth 1). Jerry perceived himself as a failed partner because he believed he had created the crisis. He viewed himself as a failed protector because he could not find a logical solution to the predicament (Myth 2). Jerry also feared that therapy would confirm the defects in his character, causing Nance to abandon the relationship (Myth 3).

Jerry and Nance had been married for eighteen years and were the parents of four children. Both described the family as being close. Their life had come to a crashing halt, however, with Jerry's guilt-laden confession of unfaithfulness. The confession had devastated Nance, and the subsequent turmoil had been negatively affecting the entire family. Jerry was perplexed as to why he had engaged in the sexual encounters, and he attributed the brief affair to his excessive drinking at an out-of-town convention. He said he still loved Nance and found her attractive and desirable. Nance believed Jerry when he told her there was no emotional connection to the other woman.

Although Jerry expressed in our session what seemed to be genuine remorse, he was adamant that he would not discuss his past. He believed that his early experiences were irrelevant to his infidelity. I assured Jerry we would not explore any areas he perceived to be uncomfortable. However, I cautioned him that this restriction might limit our understanding of the underlying causes. This was fine with him, since he perceived his affair as having been strongly linked to a character deficiency. He also reported feeling that Nance was a loving person and not at all to blame. In his eyes, he was defective and very willing to verbally punish himself as a means of absolution. He would repeatedly say in different ways that he was a terrible husband who did not deserve to have such a wonderful wife.

The first few sessions demonstrated to Jerry that we were not going to violate the boundary of exploring his past. Although progress was slow, some factors evolved that shed a new light on the surface of this seemingly solid marital relationship. It was revealed that Nance was still extremely close to her family of origin, which included seven siblings, their families, and her parents. Jerry, on the other hand, had a relatively distant relationship with his family of origin, which included his mother and father, as well as some siblings.

In addition, Nance's entire family lived close by. According to Jerry, her family played an active part in their life, and most of their free time was spent with family members. Nance considered her siblings her closest friends, and she believed that Jerry had enjoyed their time spent together. He admitted to having fond feelings for some of her family but objected to the amount of time they spent together. His preference would have been to have more time with just Nance and their children. This seemed very foreign to Nance, and she defended her choice by citing numerous instances over the years when family members had helped them. Although Jerry did not dispute what Nance reported, he remained definite about the need for more time alone with his core family. Nance promised to try to honor this request, but she was not willing to be more specific.

Shortly thereafter, Jerry reported a change of heart about exploring his past. He felt frustrated by the slow progress and said he was willing to do whatever was necessary to heal. However, he stated he would feel more comfortable doing the initial exploration in an individual session. Nance agreed, and a session for Jerry was scheduled. I decided to do experiential work with him and chose to do Eye Movement Desensitization and Reprocessing (EMDR), which has been very successful in trauma release. I use it frequently in healing childhood wounds, with wonderful results. (For more information about EMDR, see www.emdr.com.)

As we began the EMDR process, Jerry found it very difficult to follow the instructions. He reported very few images and mostly darkness. He was frustrated, although I assured him that the darkness was still communicating a valuable message. He became increasingly agitated and kept repeating, "I just can't do this. I just can't!" He insisted on ending the exercise. In a soothing tone, I instructed Jerry to let the images fade and go into the Healing Breath exercise (outlined at the end of chapter 1). I gently encouraged him to just stay with the breath and scan his body for whatever was present.

When he was calm, I asked him to close his eyes, go to a place of safety, and describe what was happening. Jerry described being dressed in work clothes with no shoes and walking on a beach by the water's edge. He was alone and reported that the surroundings were beautiful. He expressed a sense of peace, paused, and then suddenly became quite upset. He said, "She's not here." When I asked who "she" was, he replied, "My mother!"

As Jerry continued, his agitated tone transformed into sheer anger: "I'm forty-three years old, and I'm whining about my mother!" I assured him that his experience was not unusual. The validation served to soften his protective emotional wall. Suddenly, he felt a deep sadness and anger based on a sense of abandonment he unconsciously sensed from his mother. As Jerry allowed himself to open to this experience, he was overwhelmed by painful memories. He described his mother as self-absorbed and critical. She was unable to listen to his needs or make him feel like he was her primary concern. He began to sob as he recalled his long-repressed history.

After some release, Jerry's tears subsided, and we spent more time exploring his relationship to his mom. Then I asked him how this pattern of not being heard or feeling unimportant manifested in his marriage. His immediate reply was that Nance was the total opposite of his mother, and he again described Nance as a loving, caring person. He was emphatic about the personality differences between Nance and his mother. He said he had chosen Nance as his life partner because of this disparity. I acknowledged their dissimilarities yet asked Jerry to reexamine how he might perceive a pattern of rejection from Nance. At first he had no response, and then he stated it was impossible to feel rejected by her. I acknowledged his reply and then gently inquired about how he had reacted when being required to spend so much time with Nance's family. Jerry paused and then, in a surprised tone, said, "Oh my goodness, that's it! Nance's extreme devotion to her relatives, often at the expense of our family, brings up the feeling that my needs aren't being heard and that I don't matter!"

The revelation felt shocking to him, since it connected to a similar reaction he had toward his mother. Although her personality and Nance's were quite different, on an unconscious level Jerry experienced the same dynamics: Nance's actions *felt* reminiscent of his mother's behaviors. In both situations, he did not feel heard and believed he did not matter. He recounted the numerous times he had been asked to participate in Nance's family events and spend precious weekend time with them against his wishes. He even reported that they made important life choices, such as where to live, based on proximity to Nance's relatives. Even though he had discussed these issues many times with Nance, no changes had been made in how their time was spent. Therefore, his affair had been an unconscious attempt to meet his need of feeling important to a woman and cared for by her. Once this insight came to light, he and Nance were able to negotiate a more comfortable arrangement regarding time spent with her family. Nance's willingness to alter old patterns accomplished two important goals: first, recognizing and honoring Jerry's needs and, second, helping him experience that he did matter.

I also had Nance and Jerry incorporate a set of communication skills called the Dialogue Process. This is one of the key techniques from Imago Relationship Therapy, originated by Harville Hendrix. The Dialogue Process is a wonderful tool that allows couples to hear, validate, and empathize with one another. In addition, it encourages exploration of the existing blocks to authentic communication. Hendrix describes the process in the following manner:

> This exercise will train you to send clear and simple messages, to listen carefully to what your partner has to say, and to paraphrase your partner accurately. These skills will lead to clear and effective communication.

Although there were bumps in the marital road, Jerry and Nance were able to manage difficult situations successfully with the Dialogue Process and additional joint therapy sessions. A few months later, they reported experiencing a sense of closeness that neither had felt prior to the marital crisis.

We have examined three myths that can prevent you from embarking on your healing journey. Now that you have learned about these, you are ready to explore the three steps that allow healing to begin. In the next chapter we look at how to begin the process.

Exploring the Myths in Your Life

Before you do the exercise, quickly review the myths discussed in this chapter:

Myth 1: *If I really want to heal, I must take an honest look at myself, which means I will have to assume a lot of self-blame for making things such a mess!*

Myth 2: *I should be able to do this healing alone, and if I need support, it is an even greater sign to the world and to myself that there is something wrong with me.*

Myth 3: *If I begin the Emotional Wisdom process, the people I love will abandon me and I will be alone.*

Do the Healing Breath exercise described at the end of chapter 1, and upon completing the instructions, keep your eyes closed. Focus on the myth that feels the most relevant to your life. You can use more than one; however, use them one at a time. Then open your eyes and complete the following sentences with the *first* response that comes to mind, even if it appears not to make sense. Keep repeating the sentence and writing your response until you have nothing more to add:

The myth I was drawn to is relevant to my life because:

_____

_____

_____

_____

What I am really afraid of is:

_____

_____

_____

The worst that could happen if I face my fear is:

_____

_____

_____

I can make myself feel safer about this issue by doing or asking for:

_____

_____

_____

_____

Over the next few days notice the impact that the myth you have chosen is having on your thoughts and beliefs. You may be surprised to see how it has affected numerous areas in your life. Once you become aware of this, remember that these reactions are merely indicators that need to be addressed, since they contain messages for your well-being.

CHAPTER 6

First Phase of Healing: Establishing Safety

Now that you know the messages your feelings want to convey, as well as the truths that can support your growth, you are ready to begin the Emotional Wisdom healing process. There are three basic stages of healing, and the next three chapters explore these. Our focus in this chapter is the first crucial phase.

First Phase: Safety

Feeling safe can be very difficult. As discussed in chapter 2, the lack of emotional safety is generally based on negative childhood messages that cause you to feel shame and self-doubt. This makes it feel unsafe to initiate healing. As a result, entering the world of emotions is often experienced as similar to taking a journey into the terrifying unknown. As you move into this perceived dark and dangerous realm, you need direction (awareness), a flashlight (acceptance and guidance), and a map (steps to implement change).

To feel safe and counteract this negativity, three events must occur.

1. It is essential to feel you are not alone.

To feel you are not alone, it may be helpful to work with someone sympathetic and insightful. As discussed in chapter 5, this person probably needs to be a trained professional for part of your journey, although a trusted friend or a support group can be beneficial as well. The empathy and understanding of the other encourages a sense of acceptance and safety. Once you feel safe, you can begin sharing more of your inner self. Such disclosure can offer relief, as well as the realization that you are not isolated or "crazy" in what you are thinking or feeling. The acknowledgment goes a long way toward providing reassurance, comfort, and a readiness to proceed. For simplicity's sake, the friend, group, or professional you choose will be referred to as *the guide*.

2. The guide needs to honor you wherever you are in your process.

A significant example of being honored occurs when the process touches on a painful issue. At such points, you often might resist the exploration. A guide frequently would deal with this by encouraging you to "get past that stuck place." Even with a guide's best intentions in this process, you might feel goaded or humiliated. The perception of being forced often serves as a painful reminder of a caretaker's harmful treatment. On an instinctual, primitive level, you would be likely to experience the guide's behavior as an attack and, in turn, as a threat to survival. To stay safe, you might unconsciously adopt either of two main tactics to distract the guide and yourself: change the subject or avoid responding by answering any question with, "I don't know."

However, it is essential to embrace and *move beyond* the resistance. To achieve this, the guide must compassionately help you recognize that you are stuck. In reality, being stuck masks the feeling of fear. It is therefore essential that the guide show acceptance of both your stuck place and the accompanying fear. Often you would feel this demonstration of compassion as a physiological sensation—a feeling as if the guide had gently pricked an anxiety-filled balloon. This action releases your overwhelming tension, allowing you to feel a wonderful relief. In this way, part of your energy's daunting task of protecting the stuck place from potential additional hurt would finally be freed. The liberated energy could transform itself into a sense of trust. In turn, the trust would contribute to feelings of safety, which are essential for healing.

For the guide, showing compassion means honoring the resistance, not offering complacency. Once this honoring has been accomplished, the guide can ask your permission to begin by *exploring the fear,* while offering reassurance that the focus will not be on the painful issue. You would need the security of knowing that the topic would be examined *only when you reported a sense of readiness.* Often, the guide's expression of respect is what would eventually allow you to feel safe enough to move into the area you had originally perceived as terrifying.

Exploring Fear Safely: Roberta

Roberta, a professional woman in her mid-forties, came to my office because, after ten years of marriage, her husband, Steve, had asked for a divorce. She was distraught and could barely function. She was completely shocked, because she believed they were happy. Roberta described Steve as the love of her life. She desperately wanted to learn whatever was necessary to make the marriage work. It did not matter that Steve was not interested in salvaging their relationship. She felt responsible for the marital difficulties and could not perceive that her husband's behavior was in any way contributing to the problem.

I explained to Roberta that it takes two to make or break any relationship. I added that I was willing to help her, although at some point, it would be essential to examine Steve's contribution. I assured her that we would not do this until she felt ready. I stated that her reluctance to examine Steve's conduct was probably connected to some form of fear. I asked if we could at least investigate what felt so terrifying; Roberta agreed, and we began. First, I interpreted the message of fear, which, you may recall, is a threat to one's emotional and psychological survival. I asked how this information related to her anxiety. Initially, Roberta was at a loss and could not make a meaningful association. Then, suddenly, her facial expression drooped, and her body sagged. She looked as if she wanted to cry. In a barely audible voice she stated, "There is no point in exploring Steve's behavior; it's not his fault. The proof is that people are always leaving *me*." Roberta began to sob gently. After she stopped, I asked her how she felt. She wiped her eyes and replied, "I feel very sad, but it's true." She took a deep sigh and continued to dab her tears with a tissue. Her posture straightened, and she looked somewhat relieved.

I asked if she was willing to consider that self-blame had deeper implications. Roberta seemed puzzled but nodded. I asked her to recognize what else these feelings were mirroring. She looked startled, sighed, and then said, "If I acknowledge that my marriage is over, it means the marriage has failed, which in reality means *I failed*. I feel like something must be really wrong with me. I've always failed, and now I have failed again; this is another nail in my coffin of a lifetime of failures." At this point Roberta began to sob. After a few minutes, she dried her eyes. I asked how she was feeling. She replied, "I feel lots of different things. I am surprised and sad about what I've learned but also very relieved that the truth has come out." She took a deep sigh and continued, "Knowing what is at the bottom of this feels so much better. At least I know what I am dealing with." Roberta experienced a sense of safety because her resistance was honored by another. As a result, significant information could come into her consciousness. The deeper truth, which felt initially frightening, cleared a preliminary safe pathway to understanding. Over time, we worked on integrating the awareness, and deep healing began.

3. The guide should ask you to recall times when you felt secure and safe, to gently help you go beyond feeling stuck.

Memories of safety can be useful in this part of the healing process. Such recollections provide a soothing blanket of protection around fear, which is the feeling associated with a lack of safety. These memories can offer the courage to explore seemingly unsafe issues and loosen the cycle of negativity and dread. As described earlier, feeling safe allows you to transform energy—that is, the energy you had once used to protect yourself against further psychic injury can be released for exploration of your psychic injury's cause and for your eventual healing. If you do not have a safe place, the guide should ask you to imagine one in your mind's eye. If that is not possible, you could recall a brief moment that had once brought you joy. This might include childhood anticipation, such as opening presents on your birthday, or a feeling of communion with nature. If nothing came to mind, the guide could lead you back to the safety of the Healing Breath (outlined at the end of chapter 1). Wherever they originate, such memories are key in helping you to deal with seemingly unsafe issues.

Recalling Painful Memories from a Safe Place: Stephanie

When she came to my office, Stephanie, an attractive single woman in her late thirties, was distraught over the breakup of a long-term love affair. The termination of the relationship was totally her partner's choice. As Stephanie worked on relationship issues, a theme quickly emerged. She revealed a longstanding feeling of defectiveness. This feeling stemmed from her belief that her mother did not want her. As proof, she recalled frequently being sent to her grandfather's home. This displacement sharply contrasted with her sister's experience of always remaining at home with their mother.

A sense of defectiveness plagued every aspect of Stephanie's present life. Although she took great pains to create a "together" image in terms of her physical appearance and social skills, in reality, she felt isolated and lonely. Stephanie was mistrustful and fearful of others. Since she had few friends, the relationship breakup was particularly devastating.

Although Stephanie had an understanding of where these negative beliefs originated, the information was only somewhat helpful. For this reason, I suggested some experiential work using a form of EMDR called Resource Installation (see the EMDR website, along with chapter 4, for a brief description). I like Resource Installation because it has the positive focus of installing, or introducing, a characteristic the client desires. In Stephanie's case, we chose to install a sense of self-acceptance. After doing the preparatory script, we began the experiential portion. In the first set, she described seeing total blackness but hearing yelling and screaming; she reported feeling very frightened. In the next set, she envisioned herself as a baby on a changing table with her mother standing over her. To her absolute horror, she distinctly felt her mother's hatred and overwhelming desire to kill her. The feelings were so intense that Stephanie began sobbing and asked that we end the exercise. We did, although her crying continued.

After the emotional release subsided, she discussed the profound effect the images were having on her. Stephanie said, "I guess my mother was right—I am not somebody worthy of being loved!" I gently asked her if there ever was someone who made her feel different and safe. At first she paused and then, with a slight smile, replied, "My grandfather." She described him as a very loving, patient man. I asked if there was a particularly soothing scene she could remember. Almost immediately she told me about the times she had spent visiting with him. I asked her to concentrate on those memories. I proposed completing the Resource Installation while focusing on those positive recollections. She said she was willing to try.

When we resumed the exercise, Stephanie immediately went to a room where she spent time together with her grandfather. She saw herself combing his hair and placing hair ribbons on his head. She reported his good-natured acceptance of her playfulness and began smiling as she remembered the scene. In the next set she heard her grandfather's voice saying to her, "I love you just because you're you; you're a good kid." Then I asked her if she was willing to remember these pleasant memories while she replayed the earlier scene of lying on the changing table. Stephanie consented, and as she visualized the horrifying incident, she was able to re-create these positive recollections. This time, although she still felt her mother's rage, she was no longer terrified. Stephanie related to me that as she experienced her mother's intense hatred, she felt shielded by her grandfather's love. The safety of these memories defused the frightening feelings.

As the exercise progressed, Stephanie was shocked to realize that she actually had choices about how she viewed the events in her life. Although there was a strong early programming to feel defective and not acceptable, she was aware of a new option. Now she could reference her grandfather's unconditional love and acceptance. At the end of the exercise, I suggested that Stephanie display pictures of her together with her grandfather, as a concrete reminder of this alternative. She did just that and, shortly thereafter, reported feeling happier, empowered, and more optimistic. Although Stephanie still struggles with her self-image, we are continuing to strengthen her *choice* to be self-accepting and self-appreciative.

Emotional Differences between Men and Women

Before concluding this chapter, I wish to note one additional factor influencing emotional safety: the way men and women deal with their emotions. For this discussion, it does not matter whether these differences are genetic or imprinted by societal expectations. In his excellent book *Men Are from Mars, Women Are from Venus*, John Gray, author on relationships and personal growth, explores this topic in detail. My brief overview is simply to demonstrate how gender is related to safety; however, it is necessary to remember that there are always exceptions.

In general, men react to feelings primarily based on scientific logic; they are secure in the realm of the five senses. Generally, men think in concrete terms and direct their energy to problem solving. Men feel safe with tangible problems that have specific solutions. Emotions often make them feel unsafe because feelings are not visible or concrete and, therefore, unconsciously stir sensations of helplessness. To mask these reactions, men often dismiss or ignore their emotions. In addition, men are very reluctant to ask for help with understanding their feelings. Resorting to help from another is perceived as being weak and vulnerable. They often believe needing assistance is unmanly and is a sign of incompetence. Disclosure also makes men fearful that this information will be used against them, which makes them feel extremely unsafe. When forced to deal with emotional issues, they prefer to do so in isolation. Men often retreat to their safe place, which has been referred to as "their cave."

On the other hand, women view feelings primarily based on emotional logic. They are more likely to acknowledge the presence of psychological problems, although they may not possess the skills to solve them. They generally feel safe in admitting the need for an emotional resource. Women often deal with problem solving by communicating with others. The emphasis includes sharing details, which is sometimes as important as finding a solution. Such disclosure is generally experienced as a sign of trust and closeness. The sharing often results in a sense of empowerment. The camaraderie, exchange of ideas, and sense of not being alone serve as powerful catalysts for growth and healing. Women usually experience caring advice or suggestions as a sign that others are genuinely concerned.

Understanding these differences is important and has implications for what is likely to occur in the healing process. It is also something to be aware of within yourself, as you begin or continue your journey of self-awareness. The following exercise will help you move toward experiencing a feeling of safety. In the next chapter you can begin learning specific essential skills needed to understand your emotional messages.

Helping You Feel Safe

Sit comfortably and do the Healing Breath exercise outlined at the end of chapter 1. After surrounding yourself with the color and saying the words *in* and *out* as you breathe, begin to envision a large movie screen in your mind's eye. Note that the screen is split in half. On the right side of the screen, imagine a time in your life when you felt safe. Picture that time, and remember the details of what the safe space looked like. Be aware of your age, what you were wearing, who was with you, and how you felt. Just take a few minutes to allow yourself to be enveloped by the safety of the experience.

On the left side of the screen, envision something that feels upsetting in your present life, something that causes you concern or worry. Picture the following: the general surroundings of this worrisome situation, the role of others, as well as your own involvement. Now take the safe feelings that you experienced on the right side of the screen and surround the situation on the left side. As you do this, feel yourself empowered by the safety that you envisioned. From this place, consider the following questions, and let the answers emerge from your inner wisdom. Remember not to force any type of change in the imagery. Whatever reaction or lack of reaction you are feeling can still provide information. A nonreaction is merely an indicator that what you thought would make you safe is not really accomplishing that goal. Perhaps it would be helpful to choose another image of safety. If that does not feel possible, or if what you choose next does not work, this is merely an indicator of how embedded the fear can be. At this point, *do not blame yourself;* just develop compassion and acceptance for this truth, which is, itself, a significant first step in healing. Now let us proceed.

1. How does the feeling of safety that now surrounds the worrisome situation affect it? Does it provide a blanket of protection around the issue, or does it somehow increase your anxiety?

2. What, if anything, has changed on the left side of the screen since the feeling of safety was created? Does the issue seem less intense or less overwhelming? Has any other aspect of it been altered by feeling safe?

3. How are you feeling as you view the situation from a safe place? Do you feel less anxious or no different than before the exercise? Has your perspective changed?

4. What three *small* action steps can you create to make yourself feel safer in your daily life? These steps can be concrete or attitudinal changes. If it is helpful, refer to client cases throughout the book for some ideas.

5. Choose one of the three steps and make a commitment to begin implementing it in your life right now.

Note: Please recognize that it is okay if there is no change in the troublesome picture on the left side of the screen after you have brought in feelings of safety. Any absence of apparent change does not mean that change is not possible; it means that there is more exploration to be done! Also, if you are unable to move any positive feelings over to the left for now, that is okay as well. All these reactions are merely indicators of internal messages that need to be understood with compassion.

Review this exercise over a period of a few days and observe your reaction. Does it remain the same as time passes and you implement the action step, or does it change? If change occurs, note how the change manifests and what it conveys.

CHAPTER 7

Second Phase of Healing: Triple-A Protection Plan

The next phase of healing is a three-step plan called the "Triple-A Protection Plan." The term *Triple-A* is generally associated with car trouble. Just as you need help with your car, you may also need help in resolving longstanding personal issues. Thus, from the emotional perspective, the abbreviation *AAA* represents *awareness, acceptance,* and *action*, each of which we now explore.

Awareness

Awareness is essential to discovering the *reason* for feeling muddled and confused. Often you know something is wrong but just can't understand the cause. Pinpointing what is specifically troubling you provides a focus for healing. The information can be experienced as a huge relief. Awareness allows you to reframe a situation and examine it from fresh perspectives. New choices become available, and what you discover can move you from helplessness to empowerment.

Developing Awareness: Rachael

Rachael, a twenty-eight-year-old physical therapist, was upset with her ex-husband Jim's relationship with their two-year-old daughter, Anna. Jim was rarely willing to spend time with Anna, although he had a close relationship with their nine-year-old daughter, Amy. Anna had been born shortly after the couple's separation, and Jim had initially questioned the child's paternity. Rachael had suggested a paternity test, but Jim had refused. After two years of Jim's rejecting behavior, Rachael found the situation intolerable and experienced intense rage toward her ex-husband. She often felt that her anger was totally out of control.

Rachael wanted to understand whether there were additional factors contributing to her powerful reaction toward Jim. Emotional Wisdom work revealed that she could strongly identify with Anna's situation. As a young child, Rachael had not felt wanted by her parents, and she recalled having been placed in foster care at age five. The awareness helped Rachael realize that some of her rage toward Jim was connected to these unresolved issues. Although she remains upset by the situation, the awareness helped her more effectively manage her anger toward her ex-husband and feel more in control.

Acceptance

Once you have learned more about a specific issue, it is *essential* that you accept this truth, whatever it may be, as part of your present reality. However, as you probably know, this is not always easy. A huge stumbling block to change is the inner battle of accepting your truth. Often, you expend so much energy fighting your reality that you end up too depleted and scared to act. In addition, this struggle creates an internal barrier that prevents you from accessing inner wisdom.

The rejection of personal truth may manifest behaviorally in various forms of denial and negative choices, leading to greater problems. For instance, if a man were to gain thirty pounds, he might reject his truth by buying looser clothing to disguise the additional weight or by eating more to "stuff" the painful realization. Either form of denial, as expressed through negative choices, would provide a cycle likely to keep him trapped and miserable as he continued gaining weight.

The greatest antidote to this negative pattern is compassion, which is the basis of self-acceptance. As discussed in chapter 5, Theodore Rubin strongly emphasizes the necessity for compassion to heal. Buddhist teacher and clinical psychologist Tara Brach, in her insightful book *Radical Acceptance*, also supports this belief: "Compassion honors our experience; it allows us to be intimate with life in this moment *as it is*. Compassion makes our acceptance whole-hearted and complete." When applied to the previous example, rather than blaming himself and engaging in more self-destructive behaviors—which, sadly, is the norm—the man would need to develop compassion for himself regarding *the reasons* the weight gain had occurred. While embracing and *accepting* the reality of weight gain, he would also need to recognize the availability of alternative, more constructive outlets for his frustrations that had caused the additional thirty pounds. If he could proceed with a weight loss plan, that would be great. If not, he would need to practice compassion and patience toward himself while considering other possibilities.

Another area where compassion is crucial is when you learn about a negative behavior or thought pattern and choose to change. The general approach is to try to replace either the behavior or the thought with something positive and, if the negative pattern continues to appear, to push it aside or fight it. However, this is a common and powerful myth. *Trying to eliminate the negative without compassion does exactly the reverse and strengthens it.* Or, as the old adage states, "What you resist, persists!" The answer is to honor whatever you have done. If that does not seem comfortable, at least accept the reasons that compelled you to initiate the behavior or thought pattern.

You are probably thinking right now, "How can I honor a thought or behavior that has been so negative in my life?" The answer is simple, but you must recall two important details. First, the behavior or thought pattern you now wish to eliminate allowed you in some way to survive up to this point. Second, on the most powerful and primitive level, the unconscious is always asking, "Is this (behavior or thought pattern) safe, or is this dangerous?" It measures safety by the fact that you are still alive and able to ask the question! Therefore on the most primal level, your emotional response to maintaining negative behavior is a resounding, "Yes, I want you to stay, because this behavior has kept me alive so far." It does not matter if there are better alternatives from which to choose; decision making is done by the higher-functioning portions of the brain—the portions that deal with reason and have nothing to do with basic survival. The negative actions or thoughts will also resist being eliminated because they are so deeply embedded in your being. You have been hardwired for this behavior for such a long time. In essence, you must always remember that, like it or not, *emotions rule!*

So you may ask, "How do I escape this trap?" The answer is to *respect the behavior or thought pattern that you want to eliminate.* Remember that it has helped you survive, even if the outcome has not been positive. The negative thought or behavior seems to be saying, "What about me? I am going to stay to make sure you are safe! I have been your constant companion, and now you want to get rid of me? Not on your life!" However, when you appreciate the old pattern for keeping you alive to this point, it is recognized, and the energy around it softens. This allows you the opportunity to make a new choice. I often suggest to clients that they put the old behavior in an emeritus position—on a psychological shelf, so to speak. Here it can be validated and appreciated for having tried to assist you in two ways. First, it may have been the only coping mechanism available to you up to this point. Second, it may have helped you get through a horrendous situation during childhood. As an aware adult, you can learn that you have other options. With this Triple-A process, new alternatives become available.

To put this process into action, you must understand compassion; your understanding, however, hinges on your having experienced compassion. The most logical source for initially learning compassion is a childhood caretaker or close relative. Unfortunately, as discussed in chapter 2, most of them were primarily raised by criticism and negativity. Therefore, you may have few experiential references for compassion and thus may experience difficulty in modeling it for the next generation.

Since compassion is so infrequently experienced, many of you may not even know how it feels. Some who have felt compassion compare it to salve on a wound: it is both soothing and calming. In addition, they describe compassion as providing a level of safety and as freeing the emotional energy that had been protecting a wound. This energy no longer has to be vigilant, which allows the person to view the situation from a calmer perspective, one that is open to cognitive awareness and reframing. Remember that the higher functions of the brain, such as self-awareness and problem-solving, reside in the cortex. These cannot be fully initiated until the primitive portion of the emotional brain, the limbic system, perceives some degree of safety.

In my thirty years of practice, I have found that providing a deep and true feeling of compassion is a key element in restoring emotional well-being. It allows clients to safely reveal their deepest fears and secrets. The light of compassion transforms perceived demons into helpful guides. Although you may not be experientially familiar with compassion, the good news is that you can develop this skill later in life. If no one in your life can offer compassion, a therapist or guide can do so.

If you do not currently have a therapist or guide, there is a quick experiential method you can try. The first part is the Healing Breath outlined at the end of chapter 1, which calms and centers you. Be aware that every person is complex and carries various aspects of the self within, including child and parent. Now allow the adult portion to project empathy on the part of you that experiences the pain—that is, on your inner child. Although this may not seem easy or possible, it may help to think of treating your pain as you would any youngster who is sad and hurt. The likelihood is that you would offer comfort, not criticism, to a suffering child. Do the same for yourself.

Learning Acceptance: Craig and Susan

Craig, a successful forty-eight-year-old executive, has been married for more than twenty-five years to Susan, a forty-seven-year-old bookkeeper. They had one daughter, Cindy, a college student. The couple came to my office because of long-term marital difficulties. For most of their relationship, Susan had suffered from severe depression. It often paralyzed her ability to function in social situations and negatively affected her relationship with Craig. Although the marriage had been generally unfulfilling, Craig felt very guilty about even considering divorce. They had married young, and at that time, he did not realize Susan's profound level of despair. In addition, Susan did not then exhibit the depth of depression that would later haunt her. Thus, Craig had spent most of his life denying the effect of her despondency on their relationship. To compensate, he had created his own life, which included a satisfying job and some friends. However, Craig reported that whenever he came home, he felt himself engulfed in a sense of doom. Throughout their marriage, Craig and Susan had basically ignored the painful consequences of her depression; thus, little had changed.

The situation came to a head when Cindy witnessed a serious argument between her parents. Cindy was so upset that she left the house crying hysterically. She told her parents that she would not come home until they made a commitment to change. Craig and Susan were shocked by the intensity of Cindy's reaction; they were very devoted to their daughter and took her threat seriously. The couple finally recognized that they had spent years pushing their problems away. They knew something needed to be done, so they finally sought relationship counseling.

The initial step was to learn compassion for themselves and each other. The goal was achieved by experiential exercises and learning the Imago Therapy couple's dialogue discussed in the previous chapter. From these techniques, they developed validation and empathy for one another. This process allowed them to *accept* the reality of their situation and share information they had previously not felt safe revealing to one another. As a result, they were ready to explore their issues with hope of change.

Action

Once you understand and accept the issue, there is still one step in the process: an action step, or action plan, to implement what you have learned. Without this, the accumulated knowledge is interesting and, perhaps, theoretically helpful, but it does not offer what you want—*life change*. Taking action involves caring enough about yourself to change. As James Ray, author and lecturer, states in *The Secret*, "Your actions are your powerful thoughts, so if you do not treat yourself with love and respect, you are emitting a signal that is saying that you are not important enough, worthy enough or deserving." Be aware that the changes you make do not have to be major. A momentum has been created even if the action steps are minute; remember that each journey begins with a tiny step. No matter how small the action, it is liberating and empowering to explore something new!

A significant but frequently overlooked factor about action steps is that the steps and/or plans need to be specific. In other words, they should be concrete, observable, and measurable. The importance of specificity is illustrated in the following example. Let us assume there are relationship issues, and you want your partner to spend more time with you. Obtaining a promise that your partner will be more attentive is too vague, since what *attentive* means is open to interpretation. For you, it may mean doing more activities together, whereas for your partner it may represent calling more frequently or sending cards and gifts. Without concrete, measurable steps, you are inadvertently creating the possibility of incurring more hurt and disappointment, thereby complicating the relationship even further. Even if you are creating the action step for yourself, it is important to break it down as if you were dealing with another person. This specificity clarifies in your mind what it is you want to accomplish and precisely how to proceed.

Taking Action: Regina

Regina, a bright, educated, divorced woman in her late fifties, came to my office distraught by her mother's recent death. She felt unable to cope with the unresolved feelings evoked by her mother's passing. She admitted being emotionally stuck and therefore unable to sort out her mother's affairs. Regina experienced this intense reaction as shocking, since she reported their mother-daughter relationship as historically unhappy. She described her mother as having always been very critical of everything she did and said. Her mother had given her the constant message that she wasn't good enough and had clearly favored her older brother, Roy. The preferential treatment of one sibling over the other had caused a noticeable strain between the siblings, which continued into the present. Her mother's death also resulted in two powerful assumptions for Regina: first, their mother-daughter relationship would never be resolved and, second, she would remain forever unlovable.

What emerged after doing some experiential work was startling. Regina learned that her mother's critical behavior had stemmed from jealousy, not from Regina's defectiveness. The root of her mother's jealousy had been Regina's close relationship with her father. Her father had spent his time and money favoring Regina, often at the expense of his wife and son. In the experiential exercise, Regina recalled numerous arguments between her parents about her dad's preferential treatment toward her. Her dad had often traveled for his job; therefore, in Regina's mind, her dad had been merely a visitor in the household. Regina had perceived the love of her mother, who had been her primary parent, as crucial. On a primitive emotional level, her mother's affection had represented daily survival and potential safety.

The awareness that her mother and brother had actually been jealous initially stunned Regina. Over time this realization allowed her to reframe her childhood memories, especially of her parents. With regard to her father, Regina slowly began to internalize his love and appreciation; eventually, she began to believe that she was lovable. In terms of her mother, Regina discovered some important truths. She realized she could begin healing their relationship from her own perspective, even though her mother was no longer alive. Based on her new awareness, she gradually developed compassion for her childhood, including her mother's reactions to her.

Once Regina accepted this truth, she was able to create small action steps to empower herself. These steps included meeting her brother at their mother's home and beginning to sort out their mother's belongings. Another step was not to automatically acquiesce to Roy's wishes. Although generally flexible, Regina remained firm in her choices regarding the division and disposal of their mother's possessions. She realized that she had spent most of her life trying to get her brother's approval. She now recognized she no longer needed it. The entire process was very liberating. Regina used these positive experiences as stepping stones to other areas of her life.

Before proceeding, it is important to make one significant point. Although the three phases of healing generally happen consecutively, there are exceptions. Healing may begin with any one of them. For example, you may accept a condition or situation before you understand it, or you can take a positive action step without yet having the underlying awareness or acceptance. However, irrespective of the order, all three phases of the process are necessary for lasting change.

Now that we have reviewed all the skills of the Triple-A Protection Plan, we will follow one case example and examine each phase of the plan.

Implementing the Triple-A Protection Plan: Paul

Paul, a tall, attractive, successful marketing specialist, came to my office seeking help with relationships. As he approached fifty, Paul had two failed marriages and was experiencing his present liaisons as unsatisfactory. He admitted he was searching for a committed relationship but found himself drawn to women who were emotionally unavailable. The majority of his affairs were filled with drama and negativity.

Awareness

In the first few sessions Paul primarily shared his history, which included specifics of his past relationships. At that point,

Paul reported being comfortable in our sessions, and his relaxed body stance seemed to confirm his statement. I suggested the possibility of some experiential work to help us access the origins of the issue, and he agreed. To help Paul relax, I began with the Healing Breath, as outlined at the end of chapter 1. Once that was accomplished, I introduced an experiential exercise. I then asked him to state his frustration in a sentence. The sentence he chose was, "Why can't someone who is emotionally available love me?" I asked him to close his eyes and keep repeating the phrase. As he did, I suggested that he access early memories of someone important in his life who was not always emotionally available. Almost immediately he remembered being in the kitchen of his parents' home. He saw his parents involved in a heated argument and his mother getting ready to leave the house.

Paul said that his parents had fought constantly and that his mother frequently had gone away for a day or two to cool off. I asked him to get in touch with what he was feeling as he saw his mother leaving. He became very sad and began trembling. His response was, "My mother doesn't love me. If she did, she wouldn't be leaving." I encouraged him to ask if there was more. His voice became choked with emotion as he continued, "I must have caused this to happen…If I were a better person, none of this would have taken place…Oh, my God, I didn't realize how powerful the past is." Overcome with emotion and unable to speak, Paul put his hands over his face. After he calmed down, we reviewed the session.

Acceptance

In the next session, I asked Paul if he had any new insights. He replied, "Not really." He told me he had spent most of the week processing the previous session. However, he noted that he had become more aware of his reactions. Paul realized that he could be very critical and that this behavior affected his romantic encounters. He also acknowledged that he could allow little things to bother him disproportionately, which caused him to badger his partners. He added that he could be mean, focusing on the negative in the relationship and not allowing himself to enjoy the positive.

Paul became aware that his judgmental behavior had built an emotional wall, creating distance in his relationships. In reality, the purpose of the wall was to protect him from the underlying fear of being rejected and abandoned. Its intent was to prevent him from possibly being reinjured. He then added, "I believe at least one, maybe both, of my wives could have offered me a healthy relationship. It's *me*." His facial expression reflected surprise.

He continued, "I've had opportunities. I screwed up. I caused them to leave, with my critical attitude and overreactions. Will I ever get it right?" Paul's emotions intensified, and he was unable to go on. I compassionately reassured him that the negative dynamic was simply trying to protect him. I added that his underlying intention was not to hurt anyone but rather to create a shield against any additional pain. I repeated to him what he had said during the previous session about the power of the past and reminded him that he, like the rest of us, was held hostage by childhood issues. I assured him that the courage to understand, as well as embrace these issues and their messages would lead him to freedom. I praised him for his bravery in exploring his history and explained that he had already taken the first steps toward healing. The support and encouragement made it easier for Paul to be receptive to these insights and begin the process of acceptance.

Action

Paul knew the real test of how much he had learned would come as he reentered the world of dating. His action steps included signing up for a personal dating service and joining some online dating sites. His initial encounters were unsatisfactory. Although Paul was attracted to some women, he realized they had negative characteristics similar to those from his past. Because of his heightened awareness, he did not become involved with them. Being conscious and not pursuing potentially negative relationships were his significant action steps. Eventually he did meet Jennifer, who was caring and unselfish. Paul soon realized she was someone with whom he could have a loving relationship.

However, not surprisingly, the relationship did not always feel comfortable. After the first few months, Paul acknowledged feeling bored and disinterested. This made him sad because he was also able to recognize Jennifer's loving and supportive nature. I assured him that these feelings were normal. His new relationship did not have the harmful turmoil that had been woven into the threads of previous liaisons. The origin of these dramas stemmed from the childhood threat of his mother's leaving and Paul's fear of being abandoned. It was precisely this scenario, along with the accompanying adrenaline rush, that was absent in his new relationship. An unfamiliar and uncomfortable vacuum had been created. Once he understood and accepted this, he learned it would be his responsibility to create stimulation, if necessary, in other areas of his life. Fortunately, this aspect of the relationship quickly took care of itself. Other family members were involved in their own dramas, which soon preoccupied Paul. Jennifer's support and caring during the various crises resulted in Paul's comment, "I don't know what I would do without her!"

Paul's learning experiences and choices can be a guide as you think about how to apply the Triple-A Protection Plan in your own life. What follows is a hands-on exercise that guides you in trying out the process.

Implementing the Triple-A Protection Plan

Think of a particular, longstanding situation in your life you wish to change. It is always wise to initially choose something not of great importance and apply it in the following steps.

Step 1: Awareness

Describe the situation as it is now:

_____

_____

_____

_____

_____

My goal—how I would like to change the situation:

_____

_____

_____

What feels unsafe about changing?

_____

_____

_____

What can I do to feel safe about changing?

_____

_____

_____

Step 2: Acceptance

Once you have faced the issue, you are ready for the step of acceptance. Complete acceptance of a situation—exactly as it is—creates an openness to change.

The question: What about the situation have I not accepted *exactly* as it is?

_____

_____

_____

_____

Is it something about myself? Is it something about the past?

_____

_____

_____

Is it something about someone else? Is it something happening now?

_____

_____

_____

The question: What do you want most from this situation?

_____

_____

_____

Step 3: Action

Now your focus becomes the important task of implementing what you have learned. Remember that action steps must be observable and measurable.

The question: What action(s) can support you getting what you most want in this situation?

_____

_____

_____

_____

I commit to taking this (these) action steps by:

_____

_____

_____

_____

Now that you have learned the healing process through the Triple-A Protection Plan, you are ready to learn, in the next chapter, seven simple skills needed to resolve *any* issue you may presently have.

CHAPTER 8

Third Phase of Healing: Essential Skills for Applying Your Emotional Messages

The third phase of healing includes essential yet simple skills you can apply to any present problem or difficult situation. Along with the Triple-A Protection Plan, outlined in the previous chapter, this phase is the heart of the Emotional Wisdom process. The information will help you become aware of the emotional truths present *below* the immediate events, commonly referred to as the "drama" or "story."

The skills are a simple variation of work I often apply with clients. They are necessary in order to learn what you want, what you realistically can do to change, and how to formulate an action plan. This process allows you to accomplish your goals. You can practice these techniques by yourself or with a guide. The next section contains an outline of the skills, followed by a case example. Please note that if you uncover some painful and unanticipated material, you may benefit from discussing it with a professional. Now let us begin.

The Seven Essential Skills for Applying Your Emotional Messages

Skill 1: *Select an issue you want to improve.*

Often, individuals are more comfortable either complaining or feeling overwhelmed by a troublesome issue than working to heal it. To avoid this trap, it is wise to initially select a problem you do not perceive as the most threatening. This advice is based on the premise that you are more likely to have greater success if you do not perceive the situation as critical. In addition, the less important the issue is to you, the less investment you will have in the outcome, so your fear of failure will be significantly reduced.

The problem you select may involve work, home, family, or any significant relationship. Fully express what is troubling you. If you are doing this alone, you may find it helpful to journal or to tape your voice. Skill 1 is important because it allows you to take whatever time you need to vent. Generally, such expression contributes to a sense of relief.

Skill 2: *Summarize the issue in one or two sentences.*

Skill 2 is significant because it helps crystallize the situation. Just make sure that the sentence reflects the essence of what is troubling you.

Skill 3: *Repeat the sentence a few times, and then identify the feelings present below the statement.*

Skill 3 is essential to getting at the core issue. Recall the feeling categories from chapter 5 (anger, sadness, fear, joy, and sexuality). Identify your feelings in terms of one or more of these five feeling groups, and recognize that it is normal for you to have more than one feeling at the same time. Simultaneous feelings, which are viewed as a paradox from a scientific perspective, are natural and customary in the emotional world. Suppose, for example, that you are getting ready to move to a new town— one where you have always wanted to live. The move can concurrently make you happy about relocating to the desired location but sad about leaving your friends and familiar surroundings.

Also be aware that certain feelings generally appear together. Anger and sadness are perfect examples. Anger often serves as a mask for sadness. This is especially true if it feels unsafe to express one's vulnerability (sadness). Paradoxically, sadness can also mask anger. This occurs if it feels unsafe to express intense emotions, which are often perceived as destructive (anger). Know that simultaneous feeling messages can be valid and relevant to your situation.

Skill 4: *Decipher the messages your feelings are trying to communicate.*

These emotional messages are the keys to unlocking your truth. They provide the necessary information to improve or resolve the current issue. Look up each feeling message in chapter 5 and relate it to your situation. For example, assume that you are angry. The message of anger is about a perceived or real sense of being violated or disrespected. The meaning can be applicable in the psychological realm or the physical one, and often in both. Allow yourself to take a deep breath as you ask yourself, "How does this information apply?" At first the meanings may seem vague and unrelated to your issue. Remember, emotional messages originate from the portion of the brain that is instinctive and primitive. Sometimes the associations may initially seem vague, and it might take time until the connections are apparent. At other times the correlations will be instantaneous.

Skill 5: *Learn to feel compassion for yourself, no matter what you uncover.*

As noted in previous chapters, it is virtually impossible to proceed with the healing process if you are stuck on self-blame or self-criticism. Such actions energetically create a wall that blocks access to your inner wisdom. Paradoxically, this knowledge is the key to positive change. In order to create an atmosphere that will encourage such awareness, you need to develop self-compassion. Refer to the previous chapter for an exercise to cultivate this significant component in healing.

Skill 6: *Determine the positive outcome you want from the situation.*

Establishing a positive outcome or goal is very important. Only when you know what you want can you align positive thinking with the appropriate action steps. This combination will result in your desired outcome. Clarifying what you would like is not as easy as you think. In my many years of clinical practice, I have found that most clients have difficulty stating what they want. In general, they are much more comfortable acknowledging what they *don't want* or what is wrong. Sometimes, to arrive at the answer, they have to begin with what they don't want and then restate it positively. For example, suppose someone is unhappy in a job and feels overworked and unappreciated. That person might think, "I don't want any more responsibilities given to me" or "I'm tired of not being recognized for my efforts." The positive reframing may be, "I have to speak to my supervisor" or "I need to find a new job!"

Skill 7: *Assess what will realistically improve the situation, and then create an action step.*

Designing an intermediary action step is the key to moving toward your goal. First you need to evaluate what you can practically do to improve your circumstances. Let's use the previous work example. Although the person may want to leave that job, doing so may not be a realistic option. There could be financial concerns or poor prospects of getting another job at that time. Thus, the individual may realize that the only realistic alternative is to speak to the supervisor. To enhance this choice, the person selects an action step, such as rehearsing not only what to say but how to positively present their concerns. Remember that action steps are effective even if they are small, because the bigger the step, the greater the anxiety and the less likely it is to be acted upon.

Now that the skills have been outlined, a case history will illustrate how this process can help. To make it easier, the case example is broken down into the seven skills.

The Seven Essential Skills for Applying Your Emotional Messages: Bruce

Bruce, a handsome, single entrepreneur in his mid-thirties, came to my office because of a deep sense of unhappiness. Bruce had been in conventional talk therapy for more than a year. Although he acknowledged having learned a lot, he had not experienced any significant life changes. His demeanor was outgoing and charming, even though he had an underlying sadness. Bruce indicated that he had friends but described himself as somewhat of a loner. He had a history of long-term relationships with women, but he had terminated most of them and could not identify any significant pattern in these breakups. Bruce stated that his time was primarily occupied with business. He reluctantly conceded he was a workaholic.

Skill 1: *Select an issue you want to improve.*

At that moment, Bruce's main concern was his relationship to his mother. He was an only child, and his father was deceased.

He described his mother as both manipulative and overdramatic. She constantly portrayed herself as a helpless victim. Bruce found himself very angry at his mother's relentless demands. She depended on him to run numerous errands and to be a chauffeur for her many medical appointments. What upset Bruce was his perception that his mother was capable of doing much of this on her own.

Skill 2: *Summarize the issue in one or two sentences.*

When I asked Bruce to sum up his concerns, he paused and said, "I experience my mother as a helpless, overdramatic, manipulating woman who constantly drains me."

Skill 3: *Repeat the sentence a few times, and then identify the feelings present below the statement.*

As Bruce repeated the sentence, he got in touch with intense anger. Initially, that was the only feeling he could name.

Skill 4: *Decipher the messages your emotions are trying to communicate.*

I reminded Bruce that the message of anger is about feeling violated and disrespected. I asked him to apply the meaning to his situation. He instantly responded, "I feel constantly drained by my mother. I try to be overly positive to counteract her negativity, but as a result I feel exhausted and neglectful of my own needs!" He paused and then continued, "You know, in a strange way, if I picture the scenes with my mother, there is a sense of comedy about the whole thing. My mother is a kooky, inconsistent, demanding lady who reminds me of the mother portrayed on the television show *Everybody Loves Raymond*." He smiled wistfully.

Suddenly, Bruce said he felt tense, his facial muscles drooped, and without warning he began to cry softly. He acknowledged feeling overwhelmingly sad about his mother's weaknesses. He was also upset about portraying his mother as a "crazy person who needs help and refuses to get it." I gently reminded him that the message of sadness is about loss. I asked him to apply the meaning to his situation. Bruce immediately replied, "I feel so alone. My mother is aging and ailing, and I am terrified of losing her. She is the last family member alive who is supposed to unconditionally love me. I feel so abandoned by her on so many levels. She was supposed to take care of me and never really did. It feels as if our roles have been reversed!"

I asked Bruce why he has felt so compelled to be available to someone he described as "outrageously selfish." He replied that he didn't know. I explained that the intense tie he experienced with his mother is often related to some type of unconscious longing or need. He looked surprised. I added that the feeling associated with that need is fear. Specifically, the fear is related to *not* getting the need met. We reviewed the message of fear, which is a perceived or real threat to survival. When I asked Bruce to apply it to his situation, initially he was uncertain. Suddenly he sat up straight and said, "Oh, my goodness, I'm still looking for something from her that I never have gotten and probably never will—her focus and interest in me and my life. I need and want that so desperately. On some level, I must feel I won't be able to survive without it."

Skill 5: *Learn to feel compassion for yourself, no matter what you uncover.*

This realization was initially very difficult for Bruce. He confided that he did not feel compassionate about what he had learned. He had expected the anger, but he was shocked about accessing sadness and fear. I reassured him that these feelings were understandable and were simply trying to communicate his deepest truths. I reminded him it was important not to "kill the messenger" but instead to heed its guidance. I explained that hearing the emotional messages would be more likely when compassion was present. Therefore, I suggested that he try the techniques outlined earlier to develop compassion. We began with the Healing Breath, which calmed and centered him. When we did the inner child portion, Bruce was able to imagine himself as a little boy experiencing pain and sadness. He was momentarily overwhelmed by empathy and acceptance for himself as a young child. The understanding he accessed made him more sympathetic toward his overall situation. In turn, this made him more available to hear his truths.

Skill 6: *Determine the positive outcome you want from the situation.*

As expected, Bruce initially was able to articulate only those things he did not want. He realized that although he was willing to help his mother, he no longer wished to do so at his own emotional and physical expense. Bruce did not want to feel drained and resentful when his mother asked him to do something or talked about her unending problems and complaints. Eventually, he was able to reframe these concerns into what he desired. Bruce confided that although he wished to help his mother, he also needed a comfortable detachment from her. He wanted to feel free in choosing when he would respond to her demands. Bruce also knew he needed to focus on being more at peace with the realization that emerged: no matter what he did, he could not obtain the unconditional love from his mother he so desperately sought. Bruce recognized that he would have to develop other avenues, including expanding his own inner resources, to meet that objective. He also desired to be able to spend more time focusing on his life and pursing things that interested him, including a satisfying relationship.

Skill 7: *Assess what will realistically improve the situation, and then create an action step.*

To accomplish his goal, Bruce knew he had to alter some of his present reactions to his mother's expectations. The first one he chose was to examine whether he was comfortable doing his mother's bidding. Bruce and I devised a plan that would give him some time to do an internal check. When his mother called with some demand, he would respond with, "Let me check my schedule and get back to you." This would allow him to evaluate how invasive he perceived each request to be, so he could then respond authentically.

As a postscript, after a few weeks, Bruce was able to report that he felt much calmer when interacting with his mother. He also noted that his mother's requests did not feel as demanding. Bruce was beginning to develop the perspective he so desired.

Techniques for Effectively Dealing with Conflicts

Before concluding the chapter, I want to mention a set of techniques that helps when you are embroiled in confrontational situations. I receive a lot of questions about how to deal effectively with such circumstances. Most people fear conflicts. This is because the outcome generally results in destructive behaviors, which often cause regret and remorse. The result usually includes hurt feelings, ruptured relationships, and, often, abandonment. In the following list, the first three techniques are beneficial because they teach you how to step back, detach, and gain a fresh perspective. The other three include an adaptation of techniques found in Imago Relationship Therapy, the excellent method originated by Harville Hendrix and described in chapter 5. These three techniques involve parts of the Dialogue Process you use on yourself as a tool for awareness and acceptance. What follows is the entire process for dealing with conflict more effectively.

Take some time alone.

Make sure to remove yourself when emotions are intensifying. This is difficult but essential. If you do stay, be aware that emotions can become so powerful that they blind everyone. Potent feelings often create havoc as they crash like a tidal wave, raging and destroying. At such moments, it may take practice to say something like, "There is so much happening, I need to step back and process what is taking place." Even if you just go into the bathroom to get some perspective, it is important to remove and ground yourself. Be patient; the pull to stay and have just one more chance for the final word or to release pent-up feelings is indescribably potent. The force comes from its direct, primitive relationship to the feeling that you *must* do this or your survival will be at stake. Although such a response is difficult to implement at first, you will find that at least having the awareness that there is another possible type of reaction can be helpful.

Allow yourself to release your emotions physically.

When you are overwhelmed by intense feelings, the best thing to do is to find and focus on some type of physical outlet. This will allow you to discharge negative energy and recenter yourself. The physical release you choose will likely be determined by where and when the incident occurs. Obviously, your choice will be different at work than if you are at home. Activities such as punching a pillow, taking a long walk, doing housework, gardening, or participating in some other form of exercise are all acceptable vehicles of release. Once your emotions have sufficiently calmed down, you are ready for the next step.

Take time to rest, relax, and rejuvenate.

You need to be aware that on some level you have just been through a *perceived psychological* attack. With so much energy unleashed and a good likelihood of old wounds being reinjured, it is perfectly normal to be exhausted from this encounter. Remember, these feelings need to be honored. Whether you listen to some soothing music, take a warm bath or shower, or simply take a brief nap, give yourself time to replenish.

Review what has occurred.

Once you find yourself calmer, you should begin to review the details of what happened. This can be done verbally or through writing, or even through some artistic representation. Then reflect on what you have expressed to help clarify the incident.

Do some self-talk that explains why your reaction, even if unsuitable, made sense at one point in your life.

You may have responded to a current situation in a familiar manner that, upon reflection, may not feel very productive; however, you need to remind yourself how this response served as a survival tool in your past. The key is having awareness about your history. For example, if your response to emotional upset is to withdraw, comply, and eventually feel compromised, this may be linked to a childhood response, such as to a caretaker who would become abusive when you were assertive. Since the withdrawal reaction helped you survive in the past, your unconscious assumes that it will be the best solution in the present. You need to be able to *validate and empathize with yourself* for unconsciously choosing this response, as well as explain to yourself how it made sense at one point in the past. Give yourself the permission and understanding you would offer a distressed child. In truth, we are all like children when it comes to learning new responses to old stimuli.

Recognize that you now have new options.

Even if you are not yet able to act on new realizations, simply be aware that you are no longer trapped by the limits of your old responses. Even if you feel incapable of changing your response at the moment, it may be reassuring to know that positive alternatives for you are possible.

Your Turn: The Seven Essential Skills for Applying Your Emotional Messages

Now that the skills have been outlined, it is time to apply them to your life. To review quickly, the skills are as follows:

- Skill 1: Select an issue you want to improve.
- Skill 2: Summarize the issue in one or two sentences.
- Skill 3: Repeat the sentence a few times, and then identify the feelings present below the statement.
- Skill 4: Decipher the messages your emotions are trying to communicate.
- Skill 5: Learn to feel compassion for yourself, no matter what you uncover.
- Skill 6: Determine the positive outcome you want from the situation.
- Skill 7: Assess what will realistically improve the situation, and then create an action step.

Select an issue and go through each of the skills. You'll be amazed at how much you can learn from this seemingly simple exercise!

Making the
Changes Last

CHAPTER 9

Ten Tips for Nourishing Your Emotional Wisdom

———◆———

E*motional Wisdom: A Compassionate Guide to the Messages Hidden in Your Feelings* is intended to become a valuable ally as you proceed on your journey toward healing and wholeness. As this book comes to a close, you now have opportunities for a new beginning. As you start experimenting with and applying the principles of Emotional Wisdom, keep these ten tips in mind for enhancing your process.

Tip 1: *Be aware that all decisions are made by factoring in the cost of three components: money, time, and emotions.*

In our logic-based culture, the primary factor in decision making generally is money, or the dollar effect on choices. The premise that money is our most important currency is based on money's concrete reality: you can see, touch, and feel it. However, what is forgotten are two other equally important currencies: time and emotions. Although these are not visible to the eye, their long-range effects become evident. As discussed earlier, you are simply not accustomed to factoring unseen elements, including emotions, into your choices. However, they deserve the same consideration, since *what you don't pay for with money, you pay for with time and emotions.*

Perhaps two brief illustrations will highlight this important fact. The first is a remark I frequently hear when people are considering working on personal growth. The comment is, "The process is so expensive and time consuming." The statement does not account for the turmoil and years wasted in *not* doing emotional healing. In other words, if you do not take a proactive step to change, you will unwittingly repeat destructive choices. The high cost of time and emotions will remain, reducing you to a mere puppet as these powerful feelings continue to rule your life.

The second is reflected in the destructive pattern of feeling victimized by either individuals or circumstances. Frequently, the squandered energy and time associated with being a victim remain hidden until it's too late to rectify the damage. It is only then that you lament your wasted existence, often becoming angry and bitter. You would give *anything* for a chance to revisit your choices, no matter what the cost in time and money. Although money is revered in this culture and can buy many comforts, it cannot buy either time or inner peace. It is only when we learn to consider *all three components* that our choices can become healthier and our lives more balanced.

Tip 2: *Awareness is about learning lessons. It is not about making anyone wrong.*

You are often afraid to uncover your truth, believing that you will be blamed in some way for what you uncover. As described in chapter 2, such reproach leads to the threefold process of pain, blame, and shame. This process only serves to fuel self-anger, which disconnects you even further from your inner wisdom. On the other hand, if you can *reframe the awareness* into the process of *discovering a valuable lesson*, it becomes a skill to be developed. The information allows you to make wiser choices and minimizes the likelihood of negative behaviors recurring. Though not an easy shift, it is a necessary one.

Tip 3: *New behaviors often feel scary and counterintuitive.*

Almost everyone resists new behavior. It feels awkward because of the unconscious association of comfort and safety with familiarity. We human beings are creatures of habit, and we tend to continue counterproductive actions because the outcome, even if destructive, is known. For example, you may recall the story in chapter 4 about the young child who was maliciously injured by his mother yet demonstrated an unmistakable preference to be with her. This instance illustrates that any new behavior will feel so unfamiliar that you will unconsciously assume it cannot be the right one to adopt.

Anything unfamiliar is associated with fear. Even positive transformation is linked to anxiety and trepidation. The fear is partially based on the belief that an old pattern is going to be abruptly ripped away from you; such a potential rupture creates a void that you experience as terrifying. Old behaviors, even harmful ones, become familiar friends. You often hold tightly to them, regardless of their destructive consequences.

One of the ways to counteract this reaction is to break down the desired behavior into small, nonthreatening steps. This is important for two reasons. First, doing this makes the change less overwhelming and more manageable. Second, you are likely to perceive even a minor change as empowering because it gives you a sense of success and control. Both of these factors will help you effectively manage your level of fear. If you feel empowered, you are more likely to experiment with a new response.

Sometimes when clients are asked to choose a small step, they respond, "I can't," "I don't know," or "I'm confused." The *authentic* message in these statements is still fear. What they are really saying is, "I'm afraid, and I can't admit it to myself or to you." A guide helping such individuals could effectively handle this situation by supporting their perceptions, even if they were resisting their truth. The guide would need to await and invite their final say in describing their reality. If they were to persist in their denial, that would merely be an indicator that they were not ready to proceed. The guide would then need to be accepting and wait for them to indicate a readiness to explore their resistance. Whenever their readiness became apparent, the guide might, among other things, refer them to a discussion of the emotional message of fear, such as the one in chapter 5 describing feeling categories.

Tip 4: *Don't assume that others will understand or be receptive to your new behaviors.*

On the one hand, having assumptions is important because you otherwise would have to renegotiate the smallest details of life each day, which would be time consuming and irritating. On the other hand, assumptions are often a major stumbling block to inner peace. In his wonderful book *The Four Agreements*, healer and author Don Miguel Ruiz states that making assumptions is a key hindrance to being happy. Ruiz maintains:

> In any kind of relationship we can make the assumption that others know what we think and we don't have to say what we want. They are going to know what we want because they know us so well. If they don't do what we want, what we assume they should, we feel hurt and think, "How could you do that? You should know." Again, we make the assumption that the other person knows what we want. A whole drama is created because we make this assumption and then put more assumptions on top...All the sadness and drama you have lived in your life was rooted in making assumptions and taking things personally.

Assumptions can be a major stumbling block to transformation. You are likely to believe that if people do not respond in accordance with your assumptions, you are misunderstood and, more importantly, unloved. Thus, you unconsciously interpret people's noncompliance as a personal rejection. This reaction generally serves to discourage you from exploring new behaviors and, ultimately, transformation. Thus, it is important to examine your assumptions when things do not go as planned. You need to examine whether the unsatisfactory outcome is a true broken agreement or is based on a lack of communication.

Also be aware that rejection may not be the other's ultimate intent. As previously discussed, it is likely that on an unconscious, primitive level, changes in one person can be perceived as a threat to the other's survival. If the people who are experiencing your new behaviors unconsciously sense danger, they may do whatever is possible to undermine your response. Therefore, their reactions are not so much about you as they are about their own perceived survival. It often takes strength and courage to withstand these manipulations; however, be reminded that the rewards are well worth the effort!

An antidote to this dilemma lies in *learning to verbalize* what you need and want. When this occurs, there is no doubt about either your assumptions or the response made by the other. If the verbalized request is denied, it then becomes *your* choice how to respond. You have three options. The first is to keep the relationship the same, despite the rejection of your request. The second is to abandon the relationship. The third is to modify it, which allows you to honor yourself and yet maintain some type of contact with the other person. It is empowering to realize that *you* can select the alternative.

Tip 5: *Another's overreaction to your changes is also related to fear. It is a sign that an unresolved wound in the other has been activated.*

Fear is the primary motivator, since it is connected to your most basic instinct, survival. The function of fear is to constantly scan the environment for whatever might be perceived as a threat. Generally, you are not conscious of this primitive and powerful internal warning system, even though it governs the majority of your decisions and choices.

We can disguise our fear in two ways. The first is resistance, as represented in Jerry's case history in chapter 5. In that instance, Jerry was unconsciously terrified about his relationship with his mother. He initially refused to explore the issue as possibly contributing to his marital difficulties and intensely denied its repercussions on his present problems. It was only when he experienced extreme frustration with his slow progress that he was willing to put aside some of his resistance.

The second is an overreaction to the stimulus. You may recall that Antoinette's case example in chapter 4 illustrated what was initially interpreted as an extreme reaction to a plant. In truth, the plant only *represented* a trigger to an earlier traumatic event. Once Antoinette accepted this awareness, she could modify behaviors that others had perceived as overly sensitive, unstable, or neurotic.

Before reacting in emotional situations, it's helpful to step back from the web of intensity. That detachment will help you create coping mechanisms and make more effective choices in your response. To accomplish this, one of the best techniques is to not respond immediately to the emotional drama. This is very difficult, since your automatic instinct is to fight back with your angry words. However, the more you participate without perspective, the more likely it is that the interaction will quickly deteriorate and whatever valid points you may have will be drowned in the emotional intensity of the moment. Conversely, if you can step back by saying, "I will get back to you" or "Let me think about that," you will have the opportunity to gain perspective and proceed in an empowered way. This is not easy and requires practice, but the rewards are well worth it!

Tip 6: *Although constant distraction from your issues can be harmful, conscious distraction can be helpful.*

You have seen throughout this book how unconscious distraction proves destructive and creates an elaborate web of diversions permeating your life. As discussed earlier, such diversions cause all types of addictions to develop as you continually place importance on everything but the pain you bury within. However, an aspect of distraction that is helpful and empowering is what I call *conscious distraction*. Used wisely and consciously, distraction can help you gain perspective on an issue.

Conscious distraction means you are aware of the problem, but you consciously make a choice not to dwell on the issue for a set period of time. You make an agreement with yourself to think about the issue at a later time. For example, you can choose to go to a movie or participate in an activity, such as a hobby, with the understanding that the issue will be dealt with at a time designated by you. This signifies that you are acknowledging the problem and working on it but also recognizing the importance of a break. Often during a break, the mind is processing the issue unconsciously, so when you do go back to thinking about it, you may have obtained some fresh perspectives and even steps toward a solution. On the other hand, even during a break, obsessive thoughts can occur. However, you can gently but firmly go back to the commitment you have made as to when you will deal with the issue, and then refocus yourself on what you have chosen to do. If you can keep your agreement with yourself, your mind will understand that your promise to yourself can be trusted; over time you will be more likely to relax and take a true time out.

Tip 7: *We tend to judge others on their personalities, not their character.*

It is normal and very human to be captivated by others who seem charming, humorous, and interesting when you first meet them. Such attributes certainly can be wonderful, endearing qualities that serve as a powerful magnet for others, contribute to good times, and gain much appreciation at social gatherings. Unfortunately, you, like the rest of us, may be blinded by such personality traits and remain unaware that these characteristics sometimes mask more questionable character disorders, specifically narcissism and abusive tendencies. If this is the case, their insidious trap will eventually manifest serious problems in ongoing relationships. That is not to say, however, that *everyone* with these qualities has a questionable character. But it does take time to get to know someone and make an accurate assessment. You must observe their behaviors, choices, and level of authenticity. Patience and watchfulness are well advised. If you would like to learn more about this important issue, I recommend an excellent book written for the general public: *The Wizard of Oz and Other Narcissists: Coping with the One-Way Relationship in Work, Love, and Family,* by Eleanor Payson. In it, she skillfully identifies the various forms of narcissism and helps the reader formulate steps for dealing with narcissists more effectively.

We have seen that the process of becoming accustomed to a new behavior is about creating a sense of safety and encouragement. The remaining tips focus on this aspect of transformation.

Tip 8: *New behaviors and responses flourish in environments with support and positive reinforcement.*

Be wary of expecting to learn some new behavior or response without any difficulties. When the inevitable lapse happens, you will generally get angry at yourself. In all likelihood, you will view it as a careless mistake and, more importantly, consider yourself a failure. That is why most people become so devastated when their diets, New Year's resolutions, and exercise programs do not stay on course; they perceive no other choice but to abandon their hopes. Often, they feel doomed to their unhappy fate.

This pattern stands in stark contrast to how we view a baby mastering a new skill, such as learning to walk. There is no youngster I know who takes a few steps and continues walking without repeatedly falling down. Generally, the adults in the child's world are quite accepting of this behavior. Most adults will pick up the fallen youngster and reinforce the effort with hugs, kisses, and reassuring words. Caretakers accept that these falls are simply part of the process. However, when it comes to learning a new behavior as an adult, the assumption is that once you *intellectually understand* the need to change, the process *should be* without flaws; this is based on our logical belief that "you should know better." In truth, you need to reframe yourself as an emotional child. If you could, I am certain you would not be so harsh and judgmental in dealing with your efforts to change. You would make compassionate allowances as you struggle to learn and benefit from your "miss takes"—commonly and erroneously referred to as "mistakes"—instead of doling out harsh, critical self-judgments.

Tip 9: *New behaviors require you to be gentle with yourself.*

As discussed earlier, compassion is the most difficult and yet essential element for successfully moving you forward. It is an indispensable component to guide you into the realm of greater personal freedom and happiness. The struggle for such self-empathy makes total sense if you remember that criticisms were likely the norm when you were growing up. Some of the methods to counteract this critical voice include the modeling of compassion described in chapter 7, the Healing Breath illustrated in chapter 1, and the techniques outlined in chapter 8.

Tip 10: *Healing is a process and not an event.*

Healing is a journey with many stops along the way. It is *not* a single event or the proverbial light bulb being turned on. Most importantly, it is *not* about blame, guilt, or self-torture. In the fifteen case studies presented, what is repeatedly illustrated is the *process* of exploring and uncovering buried truths. This process allows you to experience the emotional relief you long for. Healing is really a way of learning actions and of being responsible for your actions, and being authentic with yourself and others. In essence, it is about attaining a sense of peace. The emotional learning curve is not a straight road, and yet, with its twists and turns, it is the key to personal freedom and inner connection.

A helpful hint to stay in touch with your authentic process is to check in with yourself frequently to ensure you are on track. You can do this by employing the Healing Breath exercise described at the end of chapter 1 or simply by taking one minute to close your eyes and focus on the breath going in and out of your nostrils. At the conclusion of either process, open your eyes and revisit whatever is on your mind. Do not be surprised if even this brief break leads you to a fresh perspective and perhaps even reroutes your thinking.

To assist you in your process, I am concluding the chapter by providing a guided imagery to help you get in touch with your deepest feelings around an issue of your choice. It includes many aspects of Emotional Wisdom that have been outlined in this book. You can have someone read it to you, or you can record your voice using the script below. The key to this format is that imagery bypasses the conscious mind and taps into your inner wisdom. This valuable knowledge is often hidden from our consciousness; a guided imagery such as the following one can help you access this information.

Emotional Wisdom: A Guided Imagery

Get into a comfortable place—a place where you will be undisturbed, quiet, and safe. You may sit or lie down for this exercise—whatever is best for you. Gently take in a deep breath, and then slowly let it out and stay with that release.

Now, begin to tense all your body parts. Tense your head, scalp, ears, and face. And now tense your neck, shoulders, arms, hands, and fingers. Continue and tense your back, stomach, and groin. Tense your thighs, knees, calves, feet, and toes. Tense your entire body tighter, tighter, and tighter, and then slowly release. Sink into the release of the tension, and gently let it go. Then, once again tense all the muscles and tense them tighter, tighter, and tighter. Hold and gently release once more; again, sink into the letting go—just a little deeper.

And now, lovingly surround yourself with a protective, golden-white light that will be with you throughout this exercise. This golden-white light will be the basis for the safety you now feel. Just bathe in it. Let it soothingly wash over you. Know that everything that is revealed will be for your highest good and the highest good of all concerned. At this point bring your awareness to your breath. Take a deep breath and fill your abdomen, your stomach, and your chest. As you breathe, let the breath bring you loving compassion for yourself. And as you exhale, let go of as much tension and anxiety as you are comfortable in releasing. Begin again, breathing in both love for yourself and compassion, and letting these fill your abdomen, stomach, and chest. Then gently let go, once again giving up as much tension and anxiety as you are comfortable in releasing. As you sink into the safety of the release, let yourself go just a little deeper within. Sink into the safety of the protective light surrounding you, and allow it in as much as you comfortably can.

Now, from this place of love, compassion, and safety, bring into your awareness a problem or stressful situation that is in your life. From this place of safety, you are a witness—an observer—and you do not get involved. Watch where the scene takes place. Who is present? Observe how you handle this situation or problem, and witness what your feelings are. Remember, you are protected by your place of safety and are merely an observer. Now surround this situation or problem and your reactions to it, as well as your feelings about yourself, with love and compassion. Just feel the acceptance and love surround this stressful place and observe. From this place of safety, in the role of witness to yourself and to the situation, you realize that all that happens to you happens for a reason. In other words, the problem or stressful situation is a way to teach you something you need to know or to be reminded of. With this in mind, and remembering you are surrounded by love and compassion, ask yourself gently, "What am I to learn from this?" And watch for some change in the picture—a word or image flashing, or whatever form of communication your inner self is comfortable in using. Give yourself time to be open for the message you will be given. If no message comes forth immediately, continue to surround yourself with the healing light of love and compassion. And now, recognizing that change is a process, ask yourself, "What is my first step in improving the situation or problem?" Again wait for communication of the change through a scene, a word, a sound, or whatever other means your inner self wishes to use. However, remember that if messages still do not come forth, that is okay too. Lovingly accept this and remember that the process may still seem unfamiliar. With a sense of completion, thank the imagery for what it has shared, and continue to feel love and compassion surrounding you. Slowly begin to become aware of your present surroundings. Gently bring yourself back to this place and time, taking all the time you need. And when you are ready, begin to gently move and stretch your body, and slowly open your eyes, coming back to the here and now.

Once you have returned to the present, take some time to reflect on what occurred. When you are ready, ask yourself the following questions:

What did I learn about my situation from this experience?

_____

_____

_____

What, if any, was the message for me?

_____

_____

_____

What action step is comfortable for me to implement?

_____

_____

_____

Reflect on this experience and journal about any additional thoughts and feelings. Over the next few days, reread your responses to observe any new insights that may emerge.

CONCLUSION

I t has been my privilege to reveal what I have experienced as a clinician. I wanted to share with you the miracles, both big and small, I witness daily as people take this voyage and transform themselves and their lives. Please remember above all to be gentle with yourself. You are a child of the Universe and deserve to be loved and nurtured—most importantly, by you. Also, be reminded that *change is possible*. Although the road is filled with twists and turns, ups and downs, as is the process of life itself, you *can* successfully emerge empowered and more peaceful. Be patient with yourself. It is my profound hope that this book offers insights and tools to assist you on your journey. Feel free to refer to the book and the exercises whenever you need to. They will be reliable friends, always there to cheer you on wherever you are in your process.

My warmest wishes on your journey, and Godspeed!

Reflections...

Reflections...

Reflections...

Reflections...

Reflections...

Reflections...

Reflections...

Reflections...

Reflections...

ABOUT THE AUTHOR

Dr. Harriet Haberman is a licensed clinical social worker with over thirty years in the field and more than twenty-five years in private practice. The focus of her practice is guiding each client on a personal journey toward emotional and spiritual wholeness, thereby improving the client's quality of life and creating a happier, more productive individual.

Harriet Haberman, Ph.D.

Roberto Rabanne, photographer.

Dr. Haberman has received public acknowledgment for her expertise and has been interviewed on both television and radio. She has been described as a dynamic, caring practitioner who can quickly yet gently get to the heart of an issue. A program contributor to a variety of community and private organizations, Dr. Haberman has donated her workshop time to local hospitals for more than twelve years. She has also had several articles, as well as a booklet, published.

Dr. Haberman received her Ph.D. in social work from Rutgers University. As part of her postdoctoral studies, Dr. Haberman has completed clinical training and certification in Body-Centered Transformation, Eye Movement Desensitization and Reprocessing (EMDR), guided imagery healing techniques, hypnotherapy, Imago Relationship Therapy, Radiance Breathwork, and Schema-Focused Cognitive Therapy.

A resident of northern New Jersey, Dr. Haberman is the mother of a grown daughter.

To learn more about Dr. Haberman's philosophy and training, visit www.harriethabermanphd.com.

BIBLIOGRAPHY

American Heritage Dictionary of the English Language, 4th ed. New York: Houghton Mifflin, 2000.

Brach, Tara. *Radical Acceptance*. New York: Bantam Books, 2004.

Branden, Nathaniel. *The Power of Self-Esteem*. Deerfield Beach, FL: Health Communications, 1992.

Byrne, Rhonda. *The Secret*. New York: First Atria Books; Hillsboro, OR: Beyond Words, 2006.

de Saint-Exupery, Antoine. *The Little Prince*. New York: Harcourt Brace Jovanovich, 1982.

Goleman, Daniel. *Emotional Intelligence*. New York: Bantam Books, 1997.

Gray, John. *Men Are from Mars, Women Are from Venus*. New York: Harper Collins, 1992.

Guterl, Fred. "What Freud Got Right," *Newsweek*, November 11, 2002, pp. 50–51.

Harlow, Henry F. *The Nature of Love*. First published in *American Psychologist* 13 (1958): 673–85. Reproduced online at "Classics in the History of Psychology" (psychclassics.yorku.ca).

Hendricks, Gay. *Learning to Love Yourself—A Guide to Becoming Centered*. New York: Fireside, 1993.

Hendricks, Gay, and Kathlyn Hendricks. *At the Speed of Life*. New York: Bantam Books, 1993.

Hendrix, Harville. *Getting the Love You Want*. New York: HarperPerennial, 1990.

Kornfield, Jack. *A Path with Heart*. New York: Bantam Books, 1993.

Luquet, Wade. *Short-Term Couples Therapy*. New York: Brunner-Routledge, 1996.

Payson, Eleanor D. *The Wizard of Oz and Other Narcissists*. Royal Oaks, MI: Julian Day Publications, 2002.

Rubin, Theodore Isaac. *Compassion and Self-Hate*. New York: Macmillan, First Collier Books Edition, 1986.

Ruiz, Don Miguel. *The Four Agreements*. San Rafael, CA: Amber-Allen Publishing, 1997.

Walsch, Neal Donald. *Conversations with God*. New York: Putnam, 1996.

What the Bleep Do We Know!? DVD. Captured Light & Lord of the Wind Films, Twentieth Century Fox Entertainment, 2004.

World Health Organization. Quoted in *Psychotherapy Finance*, January 2001, p. 10.

Give the Gift of

Emotional Wisdom

A Compassionate Guide to the Messages Hidden in Your Feelings

to Your Friends, Family, or Colleagues

Check www.harriethabermanphd.com, or amazon.com, or order here.

❏ **YES**, I want _____ copies of *Emotional Wisdom* at $13.95 each, plus $4.95 shipping per book (New Jersey residents please add 98¢ sales tax per book).

My check or money order for $_____ is enclosed.

Name _____

Address _____

City/State/Zip _____

Phone_____ E-mail _____

Please make your check payable and return to:

ITH Publications
96 Linwood Plaza #262
Fort Lee, New Jersey 07024-3701